Microsoft® Official Academic Course: Designing a Microsoft® Windows Server™ 2003 Active Directory® and Network Infrastructure (70-297)

Lab Manual

Kurt Hudson

PUBLISHED BY
Microsoft Press
A Division of Microsoft Corporation
One Microsoft Way
Redmond, Washington 98052-6399

Copyright © 2004 by Microsoft Corporation

Printed and bound in the United States of America.

1 2 3 4 5 6 7 8 9   QWT   9 8 7 6 5 4

Distributed in Canada by H.B. Fenn and Company Ltd.

A CIP catalogue record for this book is available from the British Library.

Microsoft Press books are available through booksellers and distributors worldwide. For further information about international editions, contact your local Microsoft Corporation office or contact Microsoft Press International directly at fax (425)
936-7329. Visit our Web site at www.microsoft.com/learning/. Send comments to *mspinput@microsoft.com*.

Active Directory, Microsoft, Microsoft Press, MS-DOS, Windows, and Windows Server are either registered trademarks or
trademarks of Microsoft Corporation in the United States and/or other countries. Other product and company names men-
tioned herein may be the trademarks of their respective owners.

The example companies, organizations, products, domain names, e-mail addresses, logos, people, places, and events depicted
herein are fictitious. No association with any real company, organization, product, domain name, e-mail address, logo,
person, place, or event is intended or should be inferred.

Acquisitions Editor: Linda Engelman
Project Editor: John Pierce
Technical Editor: Beth Cohen
Copyeditor: Ina Chang
Indexer: Ginny Bess

SubAssy Part No. X10-63125
Body Part No. X10-63127

CONTENTS AT A GLANCE

CONTENTS

LAB 1

ANALYZING THE EXISTING IT INFRASTRUCTURE

This lab contains the following exercises and activities:

- Exercise 1-1: Documenting Hardware
- Exercise 1-2: Documenting Software and Services
- Exercise 1-3: Baseline Performance
- Lab Review Questions
- Lab Challenge 1-1: Environment Variables Report
- Lab Challenge 1-2: Sc Query

SCENARIO

You are working as a consultant for Trey Research. Trey Research has a contract to help design a network and Active Directory implementation for Contoso, Ltd. Contoso, Ltd., has 5,000 client computers and 150 member server computers. These computers run a variety of operating systems, including Windows NT 4.0, Windows 2000, Windows XP, and (on some computers) Windows Server 2003. The existing administrative structure consists of three domains. One is a Windows 2000–based Active Directory domain and the other two are Windows NT 4.0–based domains.

The program management design team selected for this project consists of members of both Contoso, Ltd., and Trey Research. Andy Ruth, your supervisor from Trey Research, is leading the program management design team. Andy tells you that his team is currently stalled in the process of analyzing the existing network because they don't have enough information to complete their analysis report. Andy asks you to assist him in gathering this information for analysis. Andy then assembles a small team from the Contoso, Ltd., Help Desk and Desktop Support offices to assist you. He says that your group is the development design team and assigns you as the team leader.

Andy informs you that your first assignment is to go out and collect some additional information on the existing network structure. He says that right now there isn't enough information documented about the existing network. Andy also tells you that Holly Holt, the Chief Information Officer (CIO) of Contoso, Ltd., has more information about what is required.

You meet with Holly to learn more about the network. Holly tells you that Contoso, Ltd., does not use any central network management software package. Simple Network Management Protocol (SNMP) is not in use on any server or client on the network, so using a centralized information gathering tool wouldn't provide the information you need anyway. Holly instructs you to use the utilities that are part of the default Windows NT 4.0, Windows 2000, and Windows Server 2003 operating systems and the utilities that ship with the operating system installation CDs. She informs you that the existing documentation is lacking in several key areas. Specifically, the program management design team needs help answering the following questions:

1. Which servers on the network can be upgraded to Windows Server 2003?

2. What type of network card is each computer using?

3. What are the drive configurations on the existing computers?

4. What software applications, services, and special drivers are in use on each computer?

Holly wants your team to focus on the member server computers in each department. She says that your team members should know where to find all of the server computers in the company, but they may not know what to do when they find them. They all have user accounts that are members of the local administrators on these computers, but she is not sure that they know how to collect all of the necessary information. You need to show your team how to collect the information that the program management design team requires.

> **NOTE** This scenario and network description are entirely fictional. The purpose is to give you the feeling that you are working on a larger scale project. In this lab, you will use the classroom or lab computers and configuration to perform exercise steps.

After completing this lab, you will be able to:

■ Collect information about existing hardware on the network.

■ Gather information about existing software on the network.

■ Use the Microsoft Upgrade Advisor and System Information utilities to gather information.

■ Create a performance baseline for a member server on the network.

Estimated lesson time: 120 minutes

In this lab you may see the characters *xx*, *yy*, and *zz*. Lab directions assume that you are working on computers configured in pairs and that each computer has a number. One number is odd and the other number is even (i.e., Computer01 is the odd-numbered computer and Computer02 is the even-numbered computer). When you see *xx*, substitute the unique number assigned to the odd-numbered computer. When you see *yy*, substitute the unique number assigned to the even-numbered computer. When you see *zz*, substitute the number assigned to the computer you are working at (odd or even).

EXERCISE 1-1: DOCUMENTING HARDWARE

Estimated completion time: 30 minutes

You need to show your team how to determine which servers can be upgraded to Windows Server 2003. If they discover any hardware that is not listed in the Windows Server Catalog on the Microsoft Web site, you want to demonstrate methods for collecting additional information by using System Information or Device Manager.

> **NOTE**   Even though you are running these commands on a computer running Windows Server 2003, they will also work on Windows NT Server 4.0 and Windows 2000 computers.

Using the Microsoft Windows Upgrade Advisor

1. Log on using the default Administrator credentials.

   > **NOTE**   The classroom setup specifies the default administrator username as Administrator with a password of MSPress#1. Use these credentials unless your instructor or lab proctor specifies something different.

2. Insert the Windows 2003 Server Evaluation CD into the CD-ROM drive. If the Welcome screen automatically appears, click Exit.

3. Open the Run dialog box. Click Start and then Run. The Run dialog box appears.

4. Type **D:\i386\WINNT32 /checkupgradeonly** in the Open text box and click OK. The Microsoft Windows Upgrade Advisor appears.

> **NOTE**   The command above assumes that your CD-ROM drive letter is D:. If the drive letter is not D:, you should substitute the appropriate drive letter.

5. On the Get Updated Setup Files page, select the No, Skip This Step And Continue Installing Windows radio button, as shown in Figure 1-1. Click Next. The Report System Compatibility page appears.

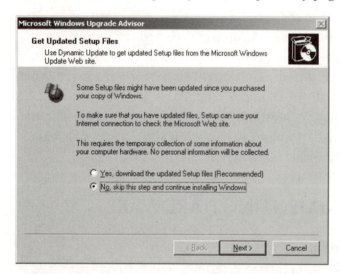

Figure 1-1   Microsoft Windows Upgrade Advisor

> **NOTE**   Since Windows Server 2003 is already installed, it is unlikely that there will be any compatibility issues. However, if there were, they would be displayed in the window and additional details concerning compatibility could be viewed by clicking the Details button.

6. Click Finish.

Using System Information

1. Open the Run dialog box.

2. Type **msinfo32** in the Open text box and click OK. The System Information utility appears.

> **NOTE**   On Windows NT 4.0 computers, use Windows NT Diagnostics. You can find Windows NT Diagnostics in the Start menu under the Programs, Administrative Tools (Common) menu options.

3. Expand the System Information utility window; you should be able to see most or all of the information in the right window pane.

4. In the left window pane, expand Components and then Network.

5. Click Adapter, as shown in Figure 1-2.

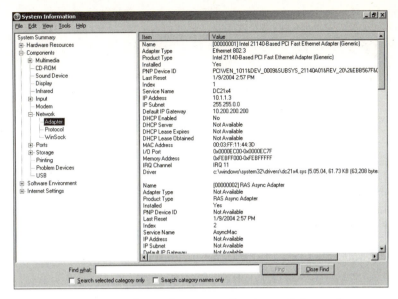

Figure 1-2   System Information network adapter information

6. Click File and then Export from the menu bar. The Export As dialog box appears.

7. Click the Save In drop down selection box, and then click Desktop.

8. Click the File Name text box, type **adapter.txt,** and then click Save.

9. Expand Storage, and then click Drives.

10. Click File and then Export from the menu bar. The Export As dialog box appears.

11. Type **drives.txt** in the File Name text box, and then click Save.

12. Close the System Information utility.

13. Open the adapter.txt file and complete the following table.

Table 1-1   Adapter information

Description	Value
Adapter Type	
IP Address	
IP Subnet	
Default IP Gateway	
DHCP Enabled	
MAC Address	
Memory Address	
IRQ Channel	

14. Close the adapter.txt file.

15. Open the drives.txt file and complete the following table.

Table 1-2   **Drive Information**

Description	Drive C: Values
Description	
Compressed	
File System	
Size	
Free Space	

16. Close the drives.txt file.

Using Device Manager

1. Click Start, right-click My Computer, and then click Properties. The System Properties dialog box appears.

> **NOTE**   In the default installations of Windows 2000 and Windows NT Server 4.0, you will find the My Computer icon on the desktop.

2. Click the Hardware tab, and then click Device Manager. The Device Manager console appears, as shown in Figure 1-3.

Figure 1-3   Device Manager on Computer03

3. Click View from the menu bar. Notice that the Devices By Type option is selected. Click Action from the menu bar.

> **QUESTION**   What options are available?

4. Click Action again to close the menu, and then click Computerzz.

5. Click Action from the menu bar.

> **QUESTION**   What options are available?

6. Click Action again to close the menu, click View, and then click Resources By Type.

> **QUESTION** When using the Resources By Type view, what information can be viewed?

7. Close Device Manager.

EXERCISE 1-2: DOCUMENTING SOFTWARE AND SERVICES

Estimated completion time: 20 minutes

Now you must show your team how to investigate any software and services running on the member server computers.

Using System Information

1. Open the Run dialog box.

2. Type **msinfo32** in the Open text box, and then click OK. The System Information utility appears.

> **NOTE** On Windows NT 4.0 computers, use the Control Panel, Add/Remove Programs applet to view installed programs. To discover startup programs, you must look in the Start, Programs, Startup folder.

3. In the left window pane, expand Software Environment and then select Startup Programs.

> **QUESTION** What programs are initiated at startup?

> **QUESTION** What user names are running startup programs?

4. Close the System Information utility.

Querying Services

1. Open a Command Prompt window. To do so, open the Run dialog box, type **CMD** in the Open text box, and then click OK.

NOTE Although the Sc utility is a default part of the Windows Server 2003 operating system, you will require an operating system–specific resource kit from Microsoft to use the command on Windows NT 4.0 or Windows 2000 computers.

2. To print a report to a text file for all services that are running on the server, type **sc query > running_services.txt** and then press Enter.

3. To print a report to a text file for all services that are currently stopped, type **sc query state= inactive > stopped_services.txt** and then press Enter. Note that a space is required after the "=" in this command.

4. To view the running services text file, type **notepad running_services.txt** and then press Enter. The open running_services document is shown in Figure 1-4.

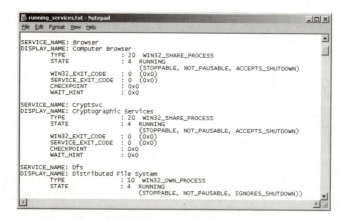

Figure 1-4   Viewing the running_services.txt file

5. To view the stopped services text file, type **notepad stopped_services.txt** and then press Enter.

6. Close Notepad when finished viewing the reports.

7. Close the Command Prompt window.

8. Open the System Configuration utility by opening the Run dialog box, typing **msconfig** in the Open text box, then clicking OK.

9. Click the Services tab.

10. Click the Hide All Microsoft Services check box.

QUESTION Are any non-Microsoft services displayed? If so, list them here.

11. Click OK to close the System Configuration utility

Checking for Unsigned Drivers

1. Open the Run dialog box.

2. Type **sigverif** in the Open text box, and then click OK. The File Signature Verification dialog box appears, as shown in Figure 1-5.

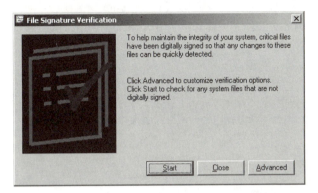

Figure 1-5   File Signature Verification dialog box.

3. To check for any system files that are not digitally signed, click Start.

> **NOTE**   This task can take a few minutes to complete. When the file signature verification process is complete, a message box appears.

4. Click OK, and then click Advanced. The Advanced File Signature Verification Settings dialog box appears.

5. Click the Logging tab.

6. Click View Log

> **QUESTION**   Look at the Scan Results line. Do you have any files that are unsigned?

7. Close the Log file.

8. Click OK to close the Advanced File Signature Verification Settings dialog box.

9. Click Close to close the File Signature Verification dialog box.

EXERCISE 1-3: BASELINE PERFORMANCE

Estimated completion time: 20 minutes

Now that your development design team is working on gathering information, Andy Ruth asks you to take on another task. He wants you to help the test design team prepare to gather baseline statistics on the upgraded member servers. The team is preparing to conduct several trial upgrades using selected Windows 2000 Server computers. After this, they will conduct testing on several Windows NT Server 4.0 computers. The team already has baseline performance statistics on how the computers running Windows 2000 Server and Windows NT Server 4.0 perform on the existing network. What they need is instructions on how to gather these same baseline statistics on the newly upgraded Windows Server 2003 computers.

The test design team needs to gather the information shown in Table 1-3. In this exercise, you will create a Counter log to demonstrate how the test design team can gather this information after the trial upgrades are complete.

Table 1-3 Performance Information

Performance Object	Counters	Instance
Processor	% Total Processor Time	_Total
System	Processor Queue Length	
Memory	Pages/sec	
Memory	Available Bytes	
LogicalDisk	% Free Space	_Total
LogicalDisk	% Disk Time	_Total
PhysicalDisk	Avg. Disk Queue Length	_Total
Redirector	Network Errors/sec	
Network Interface	Output Queue Length	Select the counter that identifies your primary network card (not loopback)

Performance Console

1. Open the Performance console. Click Start, Administrative Tools, and then Performance. The Performance console appears.

2. In the left window pane, expand Performance Logs And Alerts.

3. In the left window pane, right-click Counter Logs and then click New Log Settings. A New Log Settings dialog box appears.

4. Type **Baseline** in the Name text box, and then click OK. The Baseline dialog box appears.

5. Click Add Counters. The Add Counters dialog box appears.

6. To add the % Total Processor Time counter, click Add.

7. To add the Processor Queue Length counter, click the Performance Object selection box and then select System. Just below the Select Counters From List radio button, a list of available counters is displayed for the System performance object. Scroll down the list until Processor Queue Length appears. Select Processor Queue Length, and then click Add.

8. Using the method shown in the previous step, add the remaining object counters listed in Table 1-3. Close the Add Counters dialog box.

9. Configure the Sample Data Interval to be a one-second interval, as shown in Figure 1-6.

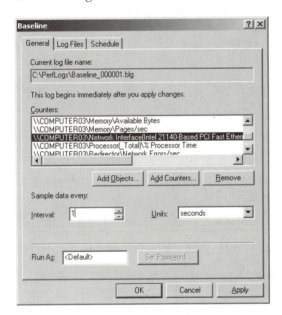

Figure 1-6 Performance counters

10. Click the Log Files tab, and then click the End File Name With drop-down selection box and select yyyymmdd.

11. Click OK. A Baseline message box appears telling you that the C:\Perf-Logs folder was not found. You are then asked if you would like to create it now. Click Yes. The Baseline log starts. Select Counter Logs in the left window pane and then the Baseline object in the right window pane.

12. Wait for 2 minutes, and then right-click the Baseline object and click Stop.

13. Click System Monitor in the left window pane. The Performance graph appears in the right window pane.

14. To clear the counter set, press CTRL+E.

15. To view log data, press CTRL+L. The System Monitor Properties dialog box appears.

16. Click the Log Files radio button, and then click Add. The Select Log File dialog box appears showing all log files that have been created.

17. Select the file named Baseline_*yyyymmdd* and click Open.

> **NOTE** The portion of the log filename represented by *yyyymmdd* will be a date, which should be the current date in year/month/day format. Select the file that substitutes this date as part of the filename.

18. Click OK in the System Monitor Properties dialog box.

19. In the right window pane, right-click the empty graph and then click Add Counters. The Add Counters dialog box appears.

> **NOTE** The only counters that will be available from here are the counters that are monitored by the log file.

20. To add the % Disk Time counter, click Add.

21. Use the method explained in step 7 of this exercise to add all the counters from the available counters in the Counter log file except % Disk Time. A complete list of the counters added to the Counter log file can be reviewed in Table 1-3.

22. Click Close in the Add Counters dialog box. You will see a graphical representation of the information you gathered, as shown in Figure 1-7.

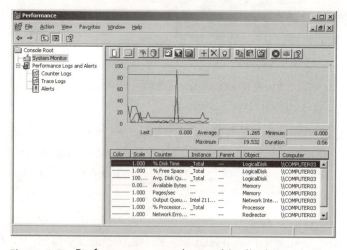

Figure 1-7 Performance console graphic display

23. You can use that method to gather and review performance information for each server on your network. Once you know the normal operational parameters, you will be able to determine whether any counters are abnormally high or low in the future. Close the Performance console.

LAB REVIEW QUESTIONS

Estimated completion time: 20 minutes

1. List methods that you can use to gather information concerning hardware on the network before you perform an upgrade from Windows NT Server 4.0 or Windows 2000 Server to Windows Server 2003.

2. List the methods that you can use to gather information concerning installed software before you perform an upgrade from Windows NT Server 4.0 or Windows 2000 Server to Windows Server 2003.

3. Use the Explain button in the Performance console to determine the acceptable threshold for the System object, Processor Queue Length counter. What is that threshold?

4. Which of the objects and counters shown in Table 1-3 can be used to indicate that there are delays on the network? What is the threshold that indicates a delay?

5. Besides the information you collected in this lab, what other information do you expect that your development design team will require in advising the program management design team on technology decisions that affect the Active Directory and infrastructure design?

LAB CHALLENGE 1-1: ENVIRONMENT VARIABLES REPORT

Estimated completion time: 10 minutes

The test design team leader, Jeff Hay, tells you that some of the Windows 2000 member server computers have custom environment variables that are required for a proprietary application they use. You need to show them how to create a report of the environment variables of these member servers for later analysis.

Task: Demonstrate how to export environment variables to a file named EnVar.txt on your local computer.

LAB CHALLENGE 1-2: SC QUERY

Estimated completion time: 20 minutes

A member of the test team, Michael Holm, informs you that certain device drivers are causing issues during the upgrade process. You need to help create batch files that will be distributed using Group Policy to collect information on these drivers.

Network Card Driver Issue

Michael tells you that a proprietary network card driver on some computers is causing upgrade problems. He is not sure how many computers on the network have this driver. Jeff Hay has requested that you help Michael compile this information. Michael has already written most of a batch file to compile this information. He just isn't sure what command to use to gather the information from the command line. You need to insert the necessary Sc command into the following batch file so that it will report information about the network card driver.

```
net  use  Q:  \\instructor01\EnVar
echo  %computername%  >>  Q:\EnVar.txt
>>  Q:\EnVar.txt
echo.
```

> **NOTE** Use *Sc /?* from the command line to help you determine the syntax for this command.

Use Sc Query to Determine the Type of Video Card Driver

Michael also tells you that some of the video card drivers in several computers have caused problems. You need to insert the necessary Sc command into the following batch file so that it will report information about the video card driver.

```
net  use  Q:  \\instructor01\EnVar
echo  %computername%  >>  Q:\EnVar.txt
>>  Q:\EnVar.txt
echo.
```

> **NOTE** The list of available options for the *group=* parameter is stored in the following Registry location: HKLM\SYSTEM\CurrentControlSet\Control\ServiceGroupOrder.

LAB 2
DESIGNING THE DNS STRUCTURE

This lab contains the following exercises and activities:

- Exercise 2-1: Analyzing the Current DNS Infrastructure

- Exercise 2-2: Analyzing the Current Administrative Model

- Exercise 2-3: Designing a DNS Deployment

- Exercise 2-4: Implementing DNS

- Exercise 2-5: Creating a Secondary DNS Server

- Exercise 2-6: Configuring DNS Forwarding

- Lab Review Questions

- Lab Challenge 2-1: Increasing DNS Security Requirements

- Lab Challenge 2-2: BIND as the Primary DNS Server

- Lab Challenge 2-3: Documenting the Network Infrastructure

SCENARIO

You are a computer consultant and are helping to implement an Active Directory and DNS infrastructure for a company named Contoso Pharmaceuticals. The company has a centralized domain structure. At this point, you don't have a lot of information about the company's IT infrastructure. You know that the company is currently using an Active Directory domain named contoso.com. You also know that the network includes several member servers.

Today, you are scheduled to attend a meeting with the CEO, CIO, and several other members of the contoso.com management team. Until now, most of the IT infrastructure maintenance was outsourced to another company. That company went out of business two months ago. While you are waiting for the meeting to start, an administrative assistant informs you that the managers were unable to gather much information about the network's administrative structure. The assistant also informs you that the meeting is delayed for two hours.

A few minutes later, the CIO arrives and asks whether you would like to have a look at some of the member servers on the network. She tells you that it would be helpful if you'd gather some additional information about the Active Directory and DNS infrastructure. She can only grant you access to the member servers at this time, but she hopes that this will let you gather at least some useful information for the meeting.

After completing this lab, you will be able to:

- Analyze DNS interoperability requirements.
- Analyze the current network administration and domain model.
- Analyze the current DNS infrastructure and namespace.
- Identify the number and location of domain controllers on the network.
- Create the conceptual design of the DNS infrastructure.
- Create the namespace design based on organizational, registration, and Active Directory requirements.
- Specify DNS security, zone type, and server options.
- Design DNS service placement.

Estimated lesson time: 145 minutes

> In this lab, you will see the characters xx, yy, and zz. The lab exercises assume that you are working on computers configured in pairs and that each computer has a number. One number is odd, and the other number is even (e.g., Computer01 is the odd-numbered computer and Computer02 is the even-numbered computer). When you see xx, substitute the unique number assigned to the odd-numbered computer. When you see yy, substitute the unique number assigned to the even-numbered computer. When you see zz, substitute the number assigned to the computer you are working at (odd or even).

EXERCISE 2-1: ANALYZING THE CURRENT DNS INFRASTRUCTURE

Estimated completion time: 10 minutes

The CIO gives you a domain user name and password that you can use to investigate the network. She tells you that the former network administrators, from the outsourced IT company, were able to see all the domain records using Nslookup commands. You decide to start gathering information.

1. Log on to the contoso.com domain using the username studentzz. Click Options. Type **studentzz** into the User Name text box and **MSPress#1** into the Password text box. Click the drop-down selection box, select CONTOSO, and then click OK.

2. Open a Command Prompt window. (Refer to Lab Exercise 1-2.)

3. Type **nslookup -d** into the Command Prompt window, and then press Enter.

> If you see a message indicating that the query was denied, the DNS server does not allow zone transfers. If you see the message, ask your instructor or lab administrator to allow zone transfers for all computers.

QUESTION   How many DNS servers are included in the contoso.com domain?

QUESTION   Which name server is the start of authority?

QUESTION   What is the IP address of the contoso.com namespace?

4. Close the Command Prompt window.

EXERCISE 2-2: ANALYZING THE ADMINISTRATIVE MODEL

Estimated completion time: 10 minutes

You've retrieved some information about the existing DNS infrastructure. Now you want to learn more about the Active Directory infrastructure of the company. You decide to use the Active Directory Users And Computers console to learn more about the administrative model of the company.

1. Open the Run dialog box.

2. Type **dsa.msc** into the Open text box, and then click OK. The Active Directory Users And Computers console appears.

   If the Active Directory Users And Computers console opened with errors, this probably indicates a connectivity problem when attempting to access the contoso.com domain. If this error occurs, try reconnecting to the contoso.com domain. In the left pane of the Active Directory Users And Computers console, right-click the Active Directory Users And Computers object and then click Connect To Domain.

The Connect To Domain dialog box appears. Type **contoso.com** in the Domain text box, and then click OK.

3. Explore the domain structure and complete the information missing in Table 2-1.

Table 2-1   Administrative Model Key Information

Administrative Model Key Information	Answers
Is this a centralized or decentralized model?	
What type of account administration is used?	
How many domain controllers exist within the contoso.com domain?	
What namespace is used for Active Directory?	

4. Close the Active Directory Users And Computers console.

EXERCISE 2-3: DESIGNING A DNS DEPLOYMENT

Estimated completion time: 20 minutes

You've been assigned to create the DNS structure for a recently acquired subsidiary of the Contoso Pharmaceuticals organization. The administrative model for the subsidiary has not yet been determined. Contoso Pharmaceuticals management has selected a DNS name for the new company (see Table 2-2). You must design a DNS infrastructure that is fault tolerant for the new infrastructure. The requirement is that if one DNS server is unavailable, another DNS server will be able to handle name resolution requests.

The subsidiary company will be connected to the Internet through the Contoso Pharmaceuticals network. The name servers at Contoso Pharmaceuticals should primarily handle Internet name resolution. The subsidiary company also has a partner company with a different DNS domain name. The name servers of the subsidiary company must be able to resolve the DNS names of the partner company without contacting Internet name servers or name servers at Contoso Pharmaceuticals. You do not want zone transfer traffic to travel between the subsidiary and partner companies.

The subsidiary company does not have an Active Directory implementation at this time. You are expected to prepare the DNS infrastructure using two Windows Server 2003 computers. When designing the DNS infrastructure, be sure to consider the following:

- Type of DNS zones and name servers

- Name resolution forwarding requirements

For Exercise 2-3, complete the sketch shown in Figure 2-1 to illustrate the DNS infrastructure that you would recommend given the requirements. Be sure to label the following:

- Company DNS names

- Computer names

- Forwarding configuration

- Zone transfers

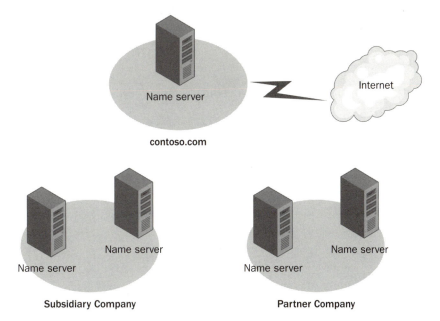

Figure 2-1   Contoso.com infrastructure

Use Table 2-2 to determine the names to use for the subsidiary company and the partner company that relate to your computer name. Computers are paired in odd/even-numbered groups for this exercise.

Table 2-2   **DNS Design Deployment**

Computer	Address	Subsidiary Company	Partner Domain Name
Computer01	10.1.1.1	adatum.com	adventure-works.com
Computer02	10.1.1.2		
Computer03	10.1.1.3	adventure-works.com	adatum.com
Computer04	10.1.1.4		
Computer05	10.1.1.5	alpineskihouse.com	blueyonderairlines.com
Computer06	10.1.1.6		
Computer07	10.1.1.7	blueyonderairlines.com	alpineskihouse.com
Computer08	10.1.1.8		
Computer09	10.1.1.9	cpandl.com	fabrikam.com
Computer10	10.1.1.10		
Computer11	10.1.1.11	fabrikam.com	cpandl.com
Computer12	10.1.1.12		
Computer13	10.1.1.13	fourthcoffee.com	humongousinsurance.com
Computer14	10.1.1.14		
Computer15	10.1.1.15	humongousinsurance.com	fourthcoffee.com
Computer16	10.1.1.16		
Computer17	10.1.1.17	litwareinc.com	lucernepublishing.com
Computer18	10.1.1.18		
Computer19	10.1.1.19	lucernepublishing.com	litwareinc.com
Computer20	10.1.1.20		
Computer21	10.1.1.21	margiestravel.com	proseware.com
Computer22	10.1.1.22		
Computer23	10.1.1.23	proseware.com	margiestravel.com
Computer24	10.1.1.24		
Computer25	10.1.1.25	southridgevideo.com	thephone-company.com
Computer26	10.1.1.26		
Computer27	10.1.1.27	thephone-company.com	southridgevideo.com
Computer28	10.1.1.28		
Computer29	10.1.1.29	wideworldimporters.com	woodgrovebank.com
Computer30	10.1.1.30		
Computer31	10.1.1.31	woodgrovebank.com	wideworldimporters.com
Computer32	10.1.1.32		

EXERCISE 2-4: IMPLEMENTING DNS

Estimated completion time: 20 minutes

You need to configure a member server of the Contoso.com domain as a primary DNS server for the subsidiary company that you will manage in the future. For now, you need to create the DNS structure in anticipation of the implementation of Active Directory in the subsidiary. You need to be sure that computers that are not a member of an Active Directory domain are able to update the DNS servers.

Use Table 2-2 to determine the correct DNS implementation for your network.

1. Log on to the odd-numbered computer as the local administrator.

2. Click Start, Control Panel, and then open Add Or Remove Programs. The Add Or Remove Programs dialog box appears.

3. Click Add/Remove Windows Components on the left side of the dialog box. The Windows Components Wizard appears.

4. Scroll down the Components list until you find Networking Services.

5. Select Networking Services.

6. Click Details. A Networking Services dialog box appears.

7. Click the Domain Name System (DNS) check box, and then click OK. The Networking Services dialog box disappears.

   Ensure the Windows Server 2003 evaluation CD is in the CD-ROM drive before moving on to the next step.

8. In the Windows Components Wizard dialog box, click Next. The selected component is installed.

9. Click Finish.

10. Close the Add Or Remove Programs dialog box.

11. Click Start, Administrative Tools, and then DNS. The DNS console appears.

12. Select Computer*xx* in the left pane, right-click it, and then click New Zone. The New Zone wizard appears.

13. Click Next. The Zone Type page appears.

14. Verify that the Primary Zone radio button is selected, and then click Next. The Forward Or Reverse Lookup Zone page appears.

15. Verify that the Forward Lookup Zone radio button is selected, and then click Next. The Zone Name page appears.

16. Type the company domain name (for example, adatum.com for Computer01) in the Zone Name text box, and then click Next. The Zone File page appears.

17. Click Next to accept the default filename. The Dynamic Update page appears.

18. Click the Allow Both Nonsecure And Secure Dynamic Updates radio button.

    If you had an Active Directory installation at this point, it would be more secure to allow secure-only updates. In this case, you have not yet installed Active Directory, so to use dynamic updates, you must allow both secure and nonsecure updates. This option allows other hosts on your network to update your DNS server without being part of your domain. The most secure options are to use only secure dynamic updates or to not allow any dynamic updates.

19. Click Next. The Completing The New Zone Wizard appears.

20. Click Finish.

21. Expand Computerzz and Forward Lookup Zones. The company domain name (e.g., adatum.com) forward lookup zone appears.

22. Select the company domain name in the left window pane, right-click it, and then click Properties. The company domain name Properties dialog box appears.

23. Click the Zone Transfers tab.

24. Verify that the Allow Zone Transfers check box is selected.

25. Select the Only To The Following Servers radio button.

26. Type the even-numbered computer IP address for the company domain name (e.g., 10.1.1.2 for adatum.com) in the IP_Address text box, shown in Figure 2-2, and then click Add.

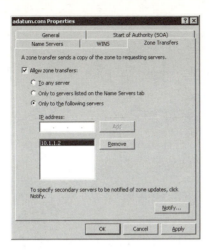

Figure 2-2 Example of Computer01 configuration allowing zone transfers to Computer02

27. Click OK.

EXERCISE 2-5: CREATING A SECONDARY DNS SERVER

Estimated completion time: 20 minutes

You need to create a secondary DNS server for the subsidiary company to implement fault tolerance.

1. Log on to the even-numbered computer as the local administrator.

2. Click Start, Control Panel, and then Add Or Remove Programs. The Add Or Remove Programs dialog box appears.

3. Click Add/Remove Windows Components on the left side of the dialog box. The Windows Components Wizard appears.

4. Scroll down the Components list until you find Networking Services.

5. Select Networking Services.

6. Click Details. A Networking Services dialog box appears.

7. Click the Domain Name System (DNS) check box, and then click OK. The Networking Services dialog box disappears.

Make sure that the Windows Server 2003 evaluation CD is in the CD-ROM drive before moving on to the next step.

8. In the Windows Components Wizard dialog box, click Next. The selected component is installed.

9. Click Finish.

10. Close the Add Or Remove Programs dialog box.

11. Click Start, Administrative Tools, and then DNS. The DNS console appears.

12. Select Computeryy in the left pane, right-click it, and then click New Zone. The New Zone Wizard appears.

13. Click Next. The Zone Type page appears.

14. Select the Secondary Zone radio button, and then click Next. The Forward Or Reverse Lookup Zone page appears.

15. Verify that the Forward Lookup Zone radio button is selected, and then click Next. The Zone Name page appears.

16. Type the company domain name (e.g., adatum.com for Computer02) in the Zone Name text box, and then click Next. The Master DNS Servers page appears, as shown in Figure 2-3.

17. Type the IP address for the primary DNS server of the company domain name (e.g., 10.1.1.1 is the primary DNS server for adatum.com; refer to Table 2-2) in the IP address text box, and then click Add.

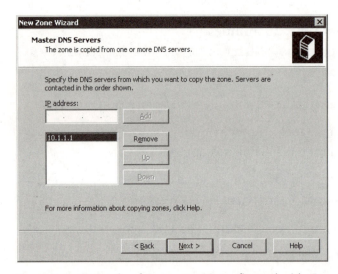

Figure 2-3   Example of Computer02 configured with Computer01 as a master DNS server

18. Click Next. The Completing The New Zone Wizard appears.

19. Click Finish.

20. Expand Computeryy and Forward Lookup Zones. The company domain name (e.g., adatum.com for Computer02; refer to Table 2-2) forward lookup zone appears in the left window pane.

    For the DNS forward lookup zone records to be transferred to the secondary DNS server, the odd-numbered computer paired to the company domain name for the even-numbered computer must be running and zone transfers must be enabled.

21. Click the company domain name (e.g., adatum.com for Computer02; refer to Table 2-2) and verify the zone transfers.

> Zone transfers are confirmed if the SOA and name server (NS) records are viewable.

EXERCISE 2-6: CONFIGURING DNS FORWARDING

Estimated completion time: 10 minutes.

You need to configure DNS forwarding appropriately for the name servers of your subsidiary company. Two main steps are required when configuring DNS forwarding in this situation. First, you must configure selective forwarding to the name servers of your partner domain for the DNS domain name of your partner domain. Second, you must configure forwarding for all other domain name requests to the contoso.com name server.

1. Right-click Computerzz in the left pane, and then click Properties.

2. Click the Forwarders tab.

3. Type **10.1.1.200** in the Selected Domain's Forwarder IP_Address List, and then click Add. This setting will forward unanswered DNS queries to the instructor DNS server.

4. Click New. A New Forwarder dialog box appears.

5. Type the partner domain name (e.g., adventure-works.com for Computer01 or Computer02; refer to Table 2-2) into the DNS Domain text box, and then click OK.

6. Type the partner domain's primary DNS server IP address into the Selected Domain's Forwarder IP_Address List, and then click Add. This setting will forward DNS queries for the partner domain to the primary DNS server of the domain.

7. Type the partner domain's secondary DNS server IP address into the Selected Domain's Forwarder IP_Address List, and then click Add. This setting will forward DNS queries for the partner domain to the secondary DNS server of the domain and provide fault tolerance. Figure 2-4 shows the completed dialog box.

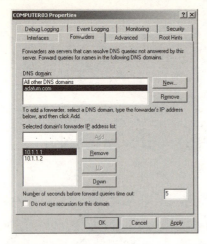

Figure 2-4   Example of Computer03 selectively forwarding requests for adatum.com.

8. Click OK.

9. Close the DNS console.

LAB REVIEW QUESTIONS

Estimated completion time: 25 minutes

1. Assume that the contoso.com domain from the scenario at the beginning of this lab uses a BIND DNS server to maintain its namespace. You are asked to replace the BIND DNS server with a Windows Server 2003 Active Directory–integrated DNS server. You need to get the existing records from the BIND DNS server to the new Windows Server 2003 computer that is to become the Active Directory–integrated DNS server. Describe the network DNS configuration that you could use to have the BIND server transfer this information to the new DNS server.

2. If the management of contoso.com decides they need another domain name that is accessible from the Internet, which of the following would not work?

    a. fabrikam.com

    b. treyresearch.net

    c. domain.local

    d. contoso.local

3. The CIO of Contoso Pharmaceuticals wants to configure a child domain for contoso.com. Which of the following names would not meet the Active Directory and DNS structural requirements?

    a. fabrikam.com

    b. treyresearch.net

      c. child.contoso.com

      d. treyresearch.contoso.com

4. To prevent computers that are not part of the domain from automatically updating the DNS database configured on an Active Directory domain controller, what setting could you use and where would you implement this setting?

5. If you want DNS records to be automatically updated through replication instead of by zone transfers, what type of DNS zones should you configure? What are the requirements of this type of configuration?

6. If you want to prevent your local DNS servers from forwarding queries to other DNS servers or from resolving client queries, what server option could you configure?

7. What type of record must be registered with the DNS server in order for Windows 2000 and Windows XP client computers to locate Active Directory domain controllers?

8. Assuming you have a large enterprise network with multiple domains, what is the minimum number of DNS servers you should configure for each domain when you use Active Directory–integrated DNS? How should you configure the DNS client computers?

LAB CHALLENGE 2-1: INCREASING DNS SECURITY REQUIREMENTS

Estimated completion time: 15 minutes

Describe and sketch your recommended configuration for the subsidiary company discussed in Exercise 2-3 assuming Active Directory was in use for the subsidiary already and the DNS requirements included:

- Need to support only secure dynamic updates

- Need for DNS record fault tolerance

- Need for secure communication between DNS servers

LAB CHALLENGE 2-2: BIND AS THE PRIMARY DNS SERVER

Estimated completion time: 15 minutes

Describe and sketch your recommended configuration for the subsidiary company discussed in Exercise 2-3 assuming that there is a BIND version 8.4.3 DNS server maintaining the namespace of the subsidiary company. Your new requirements are:

- The BIND DNS server must remain the primary DNS server for the subsidiary namespace. The BIND server currently does not allow dynamic updates and it is not an option to change this configuration.

- Active Directory domain controllers must be able to securely update their SRV records dynamically.

- Active Directory should use the same namespace as the subsidiary company.

LAB CHALLENGE 2-3: DOCUMENTING THE NETWORK INFRASTRUCTURE

Estimated completion time: 20 minutes

Use the information you gathered in this lab and in Lab 1 to document the lab or classroom network by completing Worksheet A.17, Documenting the Network Infrastructure. This document is an actual working aid from the Windows Server 2003 Deployment Kit. You'll find the document on the Student CD-ROM in the Lab Manual\Lab02 folder as DMEUSE_17.doc.

LAB 3
DESIGNING A WINS STRUCTURE

This lab contains the following exercises and activities:

- Exercise 3-1: Designing NetBIOS Name Resolution

- Exercise 3-2: Designing WINS Servers Across the WAN

- Exercise 3-3: Designing WINS to Reduce Convergence Time

- Lab Review Questions

- Lab Challenge 3-1: Designing the WINS Proxy Agent

NOTE This scenario will not follow the classroom environment.

SCENARIO

You are the network engineer for Trey Research. Trey Research has corporate offices in Mexico City (with a staff of 200) and plants in Sydney, Australia (with a staff of 200), London, England (with a staff of 150), and Phoenix, Arizona, in the United States (with a staff of 600). The physical structure for Trey Research is shown in Figure 3-1.

The company is deploying a single Active Directory forest that has four Active Directory sites. The company is moving from a Novell NetWare environment that uses only the Internetwork Packet Exchange/Sequenced Packet Exchange (IPX/SPX) protocol suite, so IP name resolution was not an issue before.

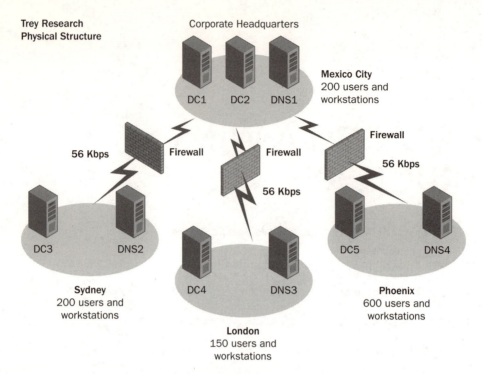

Figure 1-1 Physical structure for Trey Research

The DNS design is already implemented. There is a minimum of one DNS server in each location to enable the Windows 2000 Professional and Windows XP Professional clients to gain access to Active Directory. Currently, WAN bandwidth is only 56 Kbps and unreliable. You need to create a name resolution structure that does not add unnecessary traffic to your WAN.

Key areas for the design of name resolution and WINS will include:

■ Client operating systems running on the network

■ Server operating systems running on the network

■ Applications that use NetBIOS

■ Available bandwidth between locations that are separated by a router

■ Physical locations of client computers, servers, and applications that rely on NetBIOS

The network consists of client computers running Windows 98, Windows 2000 Professional, and Windows XP Professional. The servers run Windows NT Server 4.0 and Windows Server 2003. All applications are Active Directory aware except for two financial applications that still rely on NetBIOS.

After completing this lab, you will be able to:

- Determine whether WINS is necessary for the network
- Determine the number of WINS servers the network needs based on fault tolerance requirements
- Place WINS servers on the network to ensure NetBIOS name resolution
- Design WINS servers to optimize convergence time of the WINS database
- Develop a WINS design that spans the WAN
- Create the conceptual design of the WINS infrastructure

Estimated lesson time: 110 minutes

EXERCISE 3-1: DESIGNING NETBIOS NAME RESOLUTION

Estimated completion time: 20 minutes

You must design the name resolution strategy for the corporate office's NetBIOS needs. You need to ensure that all client computers in the corporate office can resolve all computer names, even if a single name server fails. However, you don't want to purchase any additional hardware for the network.

Referring back to Figure 3-1 and to the information provided, design the solution to this problem and draw out your solution.

EXERCISE 3-2: DESIGNING WINS SERVERS ACROSS THE WAN

Estimated completion time: 20 minutes

The network administrator now asks you to help design the WINS servers for the entire network. You decided to install WINS on the two DNS servers located in Mexico City. You need to determine how many, if any, WINS servers need to be installed in the other locations.

You discover that in the locations other than Mexico City, more client computers run Windows 98 than any other operating system. You also discover that each location has at least two Windows NT Server 4.0 computers and two Windows Server 2003 computers.

You need to ensure that all computers in the remote locations can access all other computers in the other locations by computer name and also utilize the financial applications, which reside on Windows Server 2003 computers located in Mexico City. The network administrator insists that the solution must not include LMHOSTS files.

The network administrator informs you that the WAN bandwidth between the different locations is limited.

Referring to Figure 3-1 and the information provided, sketch and describe the WINS design you would recommend.

EXERCISE 3-3: DESIGNING WINS TO REDUCE CONVERGENCE TIME

Estimated completion time: 20 minutes

Six months later, the network administrator asks you to help with a new NetBIOS name resolution design. The new NetBIOS name resolution design must accommodate the changes to the WAN bandwidth and should reduce the overall convergence time needed for the name resolution databases to synchronize their records. The new WAN link speed for each plant location to Mexico City is 5.44 Mbps. The link is very reliable and does not have any saturation issues.

You are informed that all the client computers have been upgraded to Windows XP Professional. The network administrator informs you that the servers and applications have not changed.

You need to ensure that all computers in the remote locations can access all other computers in the other locations by computer name. The network administrator insists that the solution not include LMHOSTS files. You need to reduce the number of servers and services that are running on the network.

Referring to Figure 3-1 and to the information provided, design the solution to this problem and draw out your solution.

LAB REVIEW QUESTIONS

Estimated completion time: 20 minutes

1. In Exercise 3-1, you discover that all the WINS servers are correctly deployed and the client computers are correctly configured as P-node clients with the appropriate WINS server configuration. However, when the WINS server at the client site and the WAN link are down, all clients fail to resolve any NetBIOS names. What should you reconfigure on the client computers to ensure that they can at least resolve NetBIOS computer names for the computers on their local network segment?

2. What are two methods of protecting WINS data that is sent across the network?

3. What two requirements are needed to remove WINS from a Windows Active Directory network?

4. In Exercise 3-2, you discover that the push/pull replication of the WINS database from Mexico City to the WINS server for each branch office is causing some network traffic delays during business hours. What could you do to reduce the network traffic caused by WINS replication during business hours but still allow for the WINS databases to be replicated after business hours?

5. While you are developing your solution for Exercise 3-3, you discover that not only have all client computers been upgraded to Windows XP Professional, but all servers now run Windows Server 2003. You also discover that the financial applications have been upgraded to a version that supports Active Directory. With this new information, what, if any, changes would you make to your WINS design?

LAB CHALLENGE 3-1: DESIGNING THE WINS PROXY AGENT

Estimated completion time: 30 minutes

Assume that you just completed Exercise 3-3, and then you find out that the Sydney location has 10 UNIX computers that need to access resources located on all servers. You decide to use the WINS proxy agent to help the UNIX computers resolve names of Windows computers on the network. You need to ensure that the UNIX computers can resolve computer names at every physical location. You also need to determine which computers can run the WINS proxy agent. Outline your plan to implement a WINS proxy agent to allow for name resolution with regard to the 10 UNIX computers.

LAB 4
DESIGNING THE NETWORK AND ROUTING INFRASTRUCTURE

This lab contains the following exercises and activities:

■ Exercise 4-1: Designing an IP Addressing Scheme

■ Exercise 4-2: Designing a DHCP Infrastructure

■ Exercise 4-3: Designing a Centralized DHCP Server Strategy

■ Lab Review Questions

■ Lab Challenge 4-1: Supernetting DHCP Scopes

SCENARIO

You are a consultant who has been hired to create an IP addressing design and a DHCP infrastructure design for Tailspin Toys. The Tailspin Toys domain consists of a single Active Directory domain. The physical network for Tailspin Toys is shown in Figure 4-1. Each location has both Windows 98 and Windows XP Professional client computers.

Tailspin Toys Physical Structure
tailspin.local

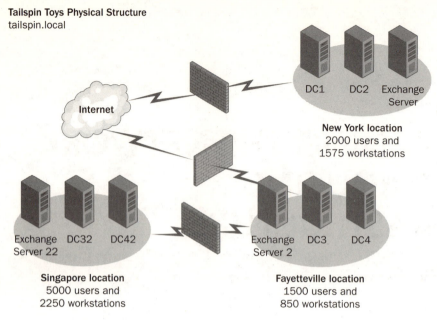

Figure 4-1   The physical network for Tailspin Toys

After completing this lab, you will be able to:

■ Specify DHCP interoperability with client types.

■ Create the conceptual design of the DHCP infrastructure.

■ Specify DHCP integration with DNS infrastructure.

■ Design a TCP/IP addressing scheme through the use of IP subnets.

■ Specify the placement of routers.

■ Design IP address assignment by using DHCP.

Estimated lesson time: 120 minutes

LAB EXERCISE 4-1: DESIGNING AN IP ADDRESSING SCHEME

Estimated completion time: 30 minutes

In this exercise, you will create an internal IP addressing scheme for all of the offices for Tailspin Toys. Your design needs to allow for the number of client computers at each location. Your plan needs to allow for future growth of at least 250 but not more than 500 clients per location. For each location, use the worksheet below to specify the ranges of IP addresses that will be used at each location.

Location	IP Address Ranges
Singapore	
Fayetteville	
New York	

EXERCISE 4-2: DESIGNING A DHCP INFRASTRUCTURE

Estimated completion time: 20 minutes

In this exercise, you will design the DHCP infrastructure and help design the routing tables for the DHCP design you created in Exercise 4-1. You need to provide a solution that allows for fault tolerance in case a DHCP server fails or if a WAN link fails. The priorities for the solution are to provide fault tolerance and keep costs as low as possible.

In the worksheet below, specify the following:

- The number of DHCP servers that will be used in each location

- How you will provide for DHCP server redundancy in each location

Location	Number of DHCP Servers	Fault Tolerance Method
Singapore		
Fayetteville		
New York		

EXERCISE 4-3: DESIGNING A CENTRALIZED DHCP SERVER STRATEGY

Estimated completion time: 20 minutes

In this exercise, you will design a DHCP strategy for a new company that Tailspin Toys has just acquired, Northwind Traders. Northwind Traders produces string and buttons. Northwind Traders only has 50 employees and 25 computers. The Northwind Traders office has a dedicated T1 leased line that connects it directly to Tailspin's New York office. You need to develop a strategy for the new DHCP design to incorporate the additional client computers. Currently, the Northwind Traders office has only a single server running Windows Server 2003. The server is operating at capacity, and Northwind Traders cannot afford a new server at this time.

What will you do to provide DHCP services to the new client computers?

LAB REVIEW QUESTIONS

Estimated completion time: 20 minutes

1. The network administrator at Northwind Traders calls you and describes a problem with the Windows 98 client computers reporting their IP configuration to DNS after they receive the IP configuration from DHCP. The solution you developed in Exercise 3 works for allocating the IP address, but the updates to DNS are a problem. You need to ensure that the DNS servers are automatically updated with the Windows 98 IP address after the DHCP server allocates it to the client computers. What should you do to the design?

2. The CIO of Tailspin Toys is concerned that if one of the DHCP servers fails, some of the client computers on the network might not be able to renew their IP address with the limited IP scopes. You need to design an alternative solution and present it to the CIO. What would be another possible solution to the split-scope design that would allow for better fault tolerance?

3. The routers located at the Northwind Traders office don't support BOOTP forwarding, and the existing Windows Server 2003 computer does not run DHCP. You don't want the existing server to run DHCP, but you do need the server to assist in the forwarding of request packets to the DHCP server in the New York office. What service will you need to install and what must you configure for the server to assist with this design requirement?

4. The administrator from Northwind Traders reports that when the network connection with New York is down, some client computers cannot communicate with any of the other computers on the network The client computers that cannot communicate with other computers on the network have an IP address of 169.254.x.x. What DHCP design changes or settings would you recommend to the administrator to help with this issue?

5. The New York office opens a new division that consists of 300 employees and 150 client computers. The CIO of Tailspin Toys wants to know whether this additional load will alter the DHCP design. Explain your answer.

LAB CHALLENGE 4-1: SUPERNETTING DHCP SCOPES

Estimated completion time: 30 minutes

If you want to reduce the configuration of the DHCP scopes by using supernetting, what would the new DHCP scopes for the following IP addressing schemes look like? Use the completed IP address table of locations and ranges below to create your answer. Be sure to include the network ID and subnet mask for each supernetted segment.

Location	IP Address Ranges
Singapore	192.168.1.1 through 192.168.1.254
	192.168.2.1 through 192.168.2.254
	192.168.3.1 through 192.168.3.254
	192.168.4.1 through 192.168.4.254
	192.168.5.1 through 192.168.5.254
	192.168.6.1 through 192.168.6.254
	192.168.7.1 through 192.168.7.254
	192.168.8.1 through 192.168.8.254
	192.168.9.1 through 192.168.9.254
Fayetteville	192.168.16.1 through 192.168.16.254
	192.168.17.1 through 192.168.17.254
	192.168.18.1 through 192.168.18.254
	192.168.19.1 through 192.168.19.254
New York	192.168.24.1 through 192.168.24.254
	192.168.25.1 through 192.168.25.254
	192.168.26.1 through 192.168.26.254
	192.168.27.1 through 192.168.27.254
	192.168.28.1 through 192.168.28.254
	192.168.29.1 through 192.168.29.254
	192.168.30.1 through 192.168.30.254

Location	IP Address Ranges	Network ID and Subnet Mask
Singapore		
Fayetteville		
New York		

LAB 5

DESIGNING THE FOREST AND DOMAIN INFRASTRUCTURE

This lab contains the following exercises and activities:

■ Exercise 5-1: Active Directory Design

■ Exercise 5-2: Active Directory Implementation

■ Exercise 5-3: Forest Trust Design

■ Exercise 5-4: Forest Trust Implementation

■ Lab Review Questions

■ Lab Challenge 5-1: Designing a Windows NT 4.0 Domain Upgrade

SCENARIO

In Lab 2, you designed and configured a DNS structure for a subsidiary company of Contoso Pharmaceuticals. In this lab, you will continue your original work to design an Active Directory structure for the subsidiary company.

Contoso Pharmaceuticals recently sold your subsidiary company to an investor group named Consolidated Messenger. Consolidated Messenger also acquired your partner company. The network infrastructure for Consolidated Messenger is shown in Figure 5-1.

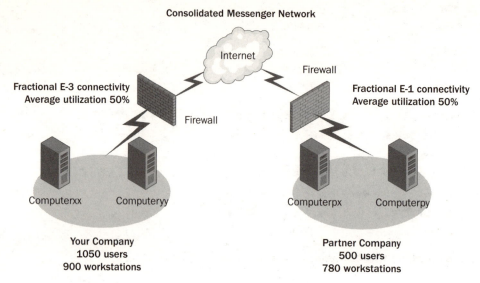

Figure 5-1   Consolidated Messenger network

Consolidated Messenger has decided to maintain the separate identity of your company as well as the partner company. However, the management of Consolidated Messenger would like to implement Windows Server 2003 Active Directory structures for both companies.

After completing this lab, you will be able to:

- Identify the existing trust relationships.

- Design the envisioned administration model.

- Create the conceptual design of the Active Directory forest structure.

- Create the conceptual design of the Active Directory domain structure.

Estimated lesson time: 225 minutes

> **NOTE**   In this lab, you will see the characters xx, yy, px, py, and zz. Lab directions assume that you are working on computers configured in pairs and that each computer has a number. One number is odd and the other number is even (i.e., Computer01 is the odd-numbered computer, and Computer02 is the even-numbered computer). The directions also assume that you have a partner company that uses a pair of computers. These computers are numbered differently, but they still use an odd-even pairing.
>
> When you see xx substitute the unique number assigned to the odd-numbered computer. When you see yy, substitute the unique number assigned to the even-numbered computer. When you see px, substitute the number assigned to the odd-numbered computer of your partner company. When you see py, substitute the number assigned to the even-numbered computer of your partner company. When you see zz, substitute the number of the computer you are working on.

LAB DEPENDENCIES

In order to complete this lab, you must have completed the following exercises:

- Implement DNS as specified in Lab Exercise 2-4.
- Configure DNS forwarding as described in Lab Exercise 2-6.

EXERCISE 5-1: ACTIVE DIRECTORY DESIGN

Estimated completion time: 30 minutes

You are assigned to the design team for Consolidated Messenger that will propose the Active Directory structure for your company and your partner company. Consolidated Messenger management has decided to limit the interaction of your company and your partner company. The CIO of Consolidated Messenger, Kim Akers, specifies the following:

- Consolidated Messenger wants data separation between the two companies. Specifically, the logical configuration of the network should not be propagated between the two companies.
- The Active Directory and Microsoft Exchange services should operate autonomously for each company.
- If a trust path is configured between the two companies, access to selected servers should be limited.

The newly appointed CIO, Steve Masters, tells the team that you must create a domain design that is fault tolerant. Steve tells you that if one server fails, you should not be forced to restore the domain from backup.

> **QUESTION** How many forests does Consolidated Messenger require? Explain your response.

> **QUESTION** How many domains do you think your company requires? Explain your response.

> **QUESTION** What is the minimum number of domain controllers you should assign? Explain.

Use Table 5-1 to document your decision on how many forests to create. Document your location and your partner company's location. In Table 5-1, list the design requirements. Add check marks to the columns indicating the isolation and autonomy requirements for your decisions (DI for Data Isolation; DA for Data Autonomy; SI for Service Isolation; SA for Service Autonomy; LC for Limited Connectivity).

Table 5-1   Forest Design Requirements

Company Name	DI	DA	SI	SA	LC

Fill out Table 5-2 based on your previous decisions. Include the domain controllers for your domain as well as your partner company's location.

Table 5-2   Domain Controller Configuration

Domain Controller	IP Address	Subnet Mask	Preferred DNS Server	Alternate DNS Server

Table 5-1 and Table 5-2 represent portions of the job aids DSSLOGI_2.doc and DSSDFR_1.doc, which you can see on your student CD under \Lab Manual\Lab05.

EXERCISE 5-2: ACTIVE DIRECTORY IMPLEMENTATION

Estimated completion time: 65 minutes

You are now expected to assist with the implementation of the design of your company's domain structure. You must configure a single forest, single domain, and two domain controllers. The odd-numbered computer will be the first domain controller installed for the domain and the even-numbered computer should be installed as a replica domain controller.

Before you begin performing the steps in this exercise, complete the right two columns of Table 5-3 by gathering information from Table 2-2, "DNS Design Deployment," in Lab 2.

Table 5-3 **Network Configuration Information**

Computer	IP Address	Company Domain Name
Your odd-numbered computer's IP address (*xx*)		
Your even-numbered computer's IP address (*yy*)		
Partner company odd-numbered computer's IP address (*px*)		
Partner company even-numbered computer's IP address (*py*)		

Configuring Preferred DNS Server on an Odd-Numbered Computer

1. Log on to computer*xx* using the local default Administrator account.

2. Click Start, Control Panel, Network Connections, and then Local Area Connection. The Local Area Connection Status dialog box appears.

3. Click Properties. The Local Area Connection Properties dialog box appears.

4. Select Internet Protocol (TCP/IP) and click Properties. The Internet Protocol (TCP/IP) Properties dialog box appears.

5. Configure your local computer's IP address as the preferred DNS server.

6. Change the alternate DNS server IP address to the IP address of computer*yy*.

7. Click OK. The Internet Protocol (TCP/IP) Properties dialog box disappears, and the Local Area Connection Properties dialog box is selected.

8. Click Close. The Local Area Connection Properties dialog box disappears, and the Local Area Connection Status dialog box is selected.

9. Click Close. The Local Area Connection Status dialog box disappears.

Installing the Forest Root Domain Controller

1. Open the Run menu.

2. Type **dcpromo** into the Open text box, and then click OK. The Active Directory Installation Wizard appears.

3. Click Next. The Operating System Compatibility page appears.

4. Click Next. The Domain Controller Type page appears, with the Domain Controller For A New Domain option selected.

5. Click Next. The Create New Domain page appears, with the Domain In A New Forest option selected.

6. Click Next. The New Domain Name page appears.

7. Type the domain name of your company (refer to Table 5-3) into the Full DNS Name For New Domain text box, and then click Next. The NetBIOS Domain Name page appears, showing the NetBIOS name in the Domain NetBIOS Name text box.

8. Click Next. The Database And Log Folders page appears, showing the paths for the database folder and log folder.

9. Click Next. The Shared System Volume page appears, showing the path for the SYSVOL folder.

10. Click Next. The DNS Registration Diagnostics page appears, as shown in Figure 5-2.

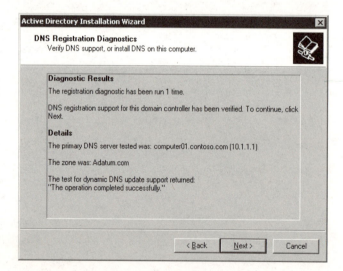

Figure 5-2 Example of Computer01 DNS diagnostic results

11. Click Next. The Permissions page appears, showing the Permissions Compatible Only With Windows 2000 Or Windows Server 2003 Operating Systems.

12. Click Next. The Directory Services Restore Mode Administrator Password page appears.

13. Type **MSPress#1** into the Restore Mode Password text box, and then retype **MSPress#1** into the Confirm Password text box.

14. Click Next. The Summary page appears, as shown in Figure 5-3.

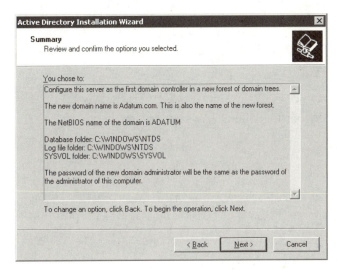

Figure 5-3   Example of Computer01 Active Directory summary information

15. Read the summary information and verify the details.

16. Click Next. The Active Directory installation procedure begins and a message appears.

> **NOTE**   The message that appears indicates that the computer account is still in the domain, even though the computer was disjoined from the domain. In a production environment, you would disable or remove the computer account. However, for this lab, don't worry about the message.

17. Click OK. The Active Directory installation procedure continues. When the installation is finished, the Completing The Active Directory Installation Wizard page appears.

18. Click Finish. A message appears.

19. Click Restart Now. The computer will perform the shutdown and startup sequence.

Configuring Preferred DNS Server on an Even-Numbered Computer

In this exercise, you will configure the even-numbered computer to use the odd-numbered computer as its DNS server. This is a similar procedure to the one that was performed on the odd-numbered computer.

1. Log on to computeryy using the local default Administrator account.

2. Click Start, Control Panel, Network Connections, and then click Local Area Connection. The Local Area Connection Status dialog box appears.

3. Click Properties. The Local Area Connection Properties dialog box appears.

4. Select Internet Protocol (TCP/IP) and click Properties. The Internet Protocol (TCP/IP) Properties dialog box appears.

5. Change the preferred DNS server IP address to the IP address of the preferred DNS server for computerxx.

6. Configure your local computer's IP address as the alternate DNS server. Figure 5-4 shows the Internet Protocol (TCP/IP) Properties dialog box for Computer02.

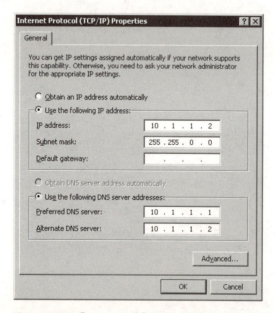

Figure 5-4 Computer02 Internet Protocol (TCP/IP) properties

7. Click OK. The Internet Protocol (TCP/IP) Properties dialog box disappears, and the Local Area Connection Properties dialog box is selected.

8. Click Close. The Local Area Connection Properties dialog box disappears, and the Local Area Connection Status dialog box is selected.

9. Click Close. The Local Area Connection Status dialog box disappears.

Installing the Replica Domain Controller

1. On computeryy, open the Run menu.

2. Type **dcpromo** into the Open text box and click OK. The Active Directory Installation Wizard appears.

3. Click Next. The Operating System Compatibility page appears.

4. Click Next. The Domain Controller Type page appears, with the Domain Controller For A New Domain option selected.

5. Select the Additional Domain Controller For An Existing Domain option.

6. Click Next. The Network Credentials page appears.

7. In the Username text box, type **Administrator**.

8. In the Password text box, type **MSPress#1**.

9. In the Domain text box, type the domain name of your company (see Table 5-3).

10. Click Next. The Additional Domain Controller page appears.

11. Type the domain name of your company (see Table 5-3) into the Domain Name text box.

12. Click Next. The Database And Log Folders page appears, showing the paths for the database folder and log folder.

13. Click Next. The Shared System Volume page appears, showing the path for the SYSVOL folder.

14. Click Next. The Directory Services Restore Mode Administrator Password page appears.

15. Type **MSPress#1** into the Restore Mode Password text box, and then retype **MSPress#1** into the Confirm Password text box.

16. Click Next. The Summary page appears, as shown in Figure 5-3.

17. Read the summary information and verify the details.

18. Click Next. The Active Directory installation procedure begins. When the installation is finished, the Completing The Active Directory Installation Wizard page appears.

19. Click Finish. A message appears.

20. Click Restart Now. The computer will perform the shutdown and startup sequence.

EXERCISE 5-3: FOREST TRUST DESIGN

Estimated completion time: 10 minutes

Kim Akers tells you to design an authentication strategy between the partner company and your company. Kim tells you that users from your partner company need to access specific resources on your domain. Kim wants to have the option of limiting the users' access to specific computers in your domain. Kim also wants this authentication path to be available to users of a child domain, should a child domain ever be added.

> **QUESTION**   What configuration would you propose to allow users from the partner company to access resources in your company? Explain your answer.

EXERCISE 5-4: FOREST TRUST IMPLEMENTATION

Estimated completion time: 45 minutes

Now you must configure a forest trust relationship between your domain and your partner company domain. You must configure this trust for selective authentication. Before you can configure your forest trust, you must raise the domain and forest functional levels to Windows Server 2003.

> **NOTE**   For this lab to work properly, you will need your company computers and your partner company computers to participate. In this case, you'll have two odd-even pairs (four computers total) completing this exercise together.

Raise the Domain Functional Level

1. Log on to computerxx using the default domain administrator's account. Close the Server Roles window if it appears after logon.

   > **NOTE**   When you log on to your computer in this exercise, ensure that you have selected your company name in the Log On To selection box. The Username should be Administrator and the Password should be MSPress#1.

2. Open Active Directory Users And Computers (click Start, Administrative Tools, and then Active Directory Users And Computers).

3. In the left pane, right-click the domain object representing your company's domain and then click Raise Domain Functional Level. The Raise Domain Functional Level dialog box appears, with Windows 2000 Native selected.

4. Use the selection box to select Windows Server 2003, as shown in Figure 5-5.

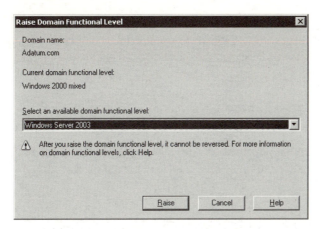

Figure 5-5 Raise Domain Functional Level dialog box

5. Click Raise. A Raise Domain Functional Level message box appears.

> **NOTE** *The message states that this change affects the entire domain and that once the domain functional level has been raised, it cannot be reversed.*

6. Click OK. A Raise Domain Functional Level message box appears.

> **NOTE** *The message states that the Domain Functional level has been raised successfully and that the new functional level will replicate to each domain controller in the domain. You are informed that the amount of time taken to replicate will vary depending on the replication topology.*

7. Click OK.

8. Close Active Directory Users And Computers.

Raise the Forest Functional Level

1. Log on to computeryy using the default domain administrator's account. Close the Server Roles window if it appears after logon.

> **NOTE** *When you log on to your computer in this exercise, ensure that you have selected your company name in the Log On To selection box. The Username should be Administrator and the Password should be MSPress#1.*

2. Open Active Directory Domains And Trusts (click Start, Administrative Tools, and then Active Directory Domains And Trusts).

3. In the left pane, right-click the object that reads Active Directory Domains And Trusts, and then click Raise Forest Functional Level. The Raise Forest Functional Level dialog box appears, showing Windows Server 2003 selected.

4. Click Raise. A Raise Forest Functional Level message box appears.

> **NOTE**   The message states that the change affects the entire forest and that once the forest functional level has been raised, it cannot be reversed.

5. Click OK. A Raise Forest Functional Level message box appears.

> **NOTE**   The message states that the forest functional level has been raised successfully and that the new functional level will replicate to each domain controller in the forest. You are informed that the amount of time taken to replicate will vary depending on the replication topology.

6. Click OK.

Create a Cross-Forest Trust with Selective Authentication

1. On the even-numbered computer, in the left pane of Active Directory Domains And Trusts, right-click the object that represents your company's domain and then click Properties.

2. Select the Trust tab, and then click New Trust. The New Trust Wizard appears.

3. Click Next. The Trust Name page appears.

4. Type the DNS name of your partner company, and then click Next. The Trust Type page appears showing the External Trust option selected.

> **NOTE**   If you see the Direction Of Trust dialog box instead of the Trust Type dialog box, click Back. Try typing the NetBIOS name (instead of the DNS name) into the Trust Name page. You can find the DNS name of your partner's domain by asking your partner to run the command **net config rdr** at a command prompt.

5. Select the Forest Trust option, and then click Next. The Direction Of Trust page appears, with the Two-Way option selected.

6. Click Next. The Sides Of Trust page appears, with The Domain Only option selected.

7. Click Next. The Outgoing Trust Authentication Level page appears with the Forest-Wide Authentication option selected. Select the Selective Authentication option, shown in Figure 5-6, and then click Next. The Trust Password page appears.

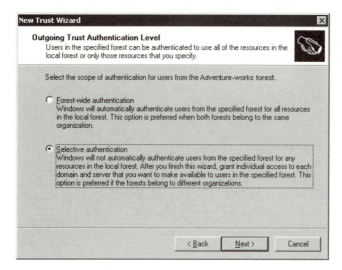

Figure 5-6   Outgoing Trust Authentication Level page

8. Type **MSPress#1** into the Trust Password text box.

9. Retype **MSPress#1** into the Confirm Trust Password text box, and then click Next. The Trust Selection Complete page appears.

10. Read and verify the information displayed, and then click Next. Another Trust Selection Complete page appears, showing the Status Of Changes.

11. Verify that the trust relationship was created successfully, and then click Next. The Confirm Outgoing Trust page appears, with the No, Do Not Confirm Outgoing Trust option selected.

12. Click Next. The Confirm Incoming Trust page appears, with the No, Do Not Confirm Outgoing Trust option selected.

13. Click Next. The Complete The New Trust Wizard page appears.

14. Click Finish. The New Trust Wizard disappears, and the Properties dialog box for your domain is selected.

15. Click OK.

16. Close Active Directory Domains And Trusts.

Allowing Partner Administrator to Authenticate

In this section, you will allow the default domain administrator from your partner company to authenticate to your domain controller. You will also create and give the partner company's default Administrator account access to this share. You must work with the students' designated as your partner company in completing this exercise. In the following steps, several notes prompt you to wait for your partner company to complete the steps before continuing. If you do not wait, the steps will not work properly.

1. On one of the computers in your odd-even pairing, open Active Directory Users And Computers.

2. On the menu bar, click View and then select Advanced Features.

   NOTE   Advanced Features View must be enabled for you to see the Security tab that allows you to change the access control list on your domain controller account.

3. Expand your domain object, if necessary. Select Domain Controllers in the left pane.

4. In the right pane, right-click computerzz.

5. Click Properties. The computerzz properties dialog box appears.

6. Click the Security tab.

7. Click Add. The Select Users, Computers or Groups dialog box appears.

   NOTE   Ensure that your partner company administrators have a chance to complete the previous steps before you move to the next step.

8. Click Locations. The Locations dialog box appears.

9. Select the domain name for your partner company (for example, Adventure-works.com is the partner company for Adatum.com), and then click OK.

10. Type **Administrator** into the Enter The Object Name To Select (Examples) text box, and then click Check Names.

    NOTE   If you complete the above step before your partner company, you are prompted to provide network credentials. This allows you to add a user account from a separate forest to the Group Or User Names list. The Username is Administrator, and the Password is MSPress#1.

11. Verify that Administrator is underlined, and then click OK. The Select Users, Computers or Groups dialog box disappears and your partner's administrator account is selected in the computer*zz* properties dialog box.

12. Select the Allow To Authenticate check box, and then click OK.

> **NOTE**   Ensure that your partner company administrators have completed the previous steps before you go on to the next step.

13. Open the Run menu and try to access the share that was created on your partner company computer. Type **\\\\IP_Address** (where *IP_Address* is equal to the IP address of the partner company computer you are trying to access). You should see a list of shares on your partner computer, including the Sysvol and NetLogon shares.

> **NOTE**   Ensure that your partner company administrators have a chance to try to access your domain before you move to the next step.

14. Return to Active Directory Users And Computers. Clear the Allow To Authenticate check box that you enabled in step 12.

> **NOTE**   Ensure that your partner company administrators have completed these steps before you move to the next step.

15. Log on as the default Administrator of your domain. Attempt to access the shared folder on your partner company domain as you did originally in step 13. You will see an error message this time indicating that you cannot access your partner company's domain controller.

LAB REVIEW QUESTIONS

Estimated completion time: 15 minutes

1. If you didn't need to use selective authentication between the partner company and your company, would you have had to raise the domain and forest functional levels to create the forest trust?

2. If your partner company was using a UNIX server and Kerberos authentication, what type of mutual authentication could have been used instead of a forest trust?

3. If Consolidated Messenger had also acquired contoso.com and decided that your partner company and your company should have child domains under the contoso.com forest root domain, what changes to your Active Directory structure would have been required?

4. Assuming that Consolidated Messenger also acquired contoso.com, how would your Active Directory structure be different if the CIO decided that all three companies should be in the same forest but maintain separate namespaces?

5. If your partner company had a Windows 2000 domain instead of a Windows Server 2003 domain, would you have been able to create a forest trust? Explain your answer. What other trust options are there, if any?

LAB CHALLENGE 5-1: DESIGNING A WINDOWS NT 4.0 DOMAIN UPGRADE

Estimated completion time: 60 minutes

John Author, director of the Baldwin Museum of Science, wants your help in upgrading his network from using a Windows NT 4.0 domain structure a Windows Server 2003 domain structure.

John explains that the museum has thousands of users and three different locations. He tells you that the primary domain controller (PDC) is in the headquarters location. There are six backup domain controllers (BDCs) on the network, two in each location. He shows you a current network diagram, shown in Figure 5-7.

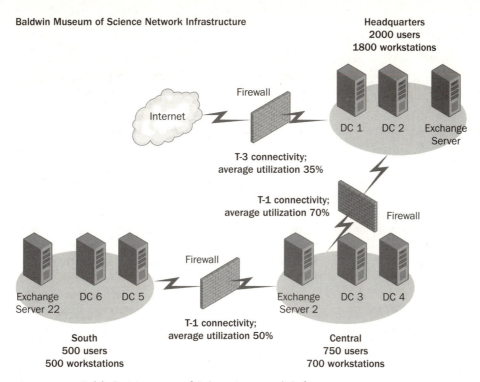

Figure 5-7   Baldwin Museum of Science network infrastructure

The organization has registered the DNS domain name baldwinmuseumof-science.com. The company has a Web presence maintained by a Web hosting provider at www.baldwinmuseumofscience.com. John tells you that the museum has no desire to host their Web site internally. They are quite happy with their Web hosting provider. However, they are eager to take advantage of the new features that Active Directory can provide over their current Windows NT 4.0 domain structure, which is shown in Figure 5-8.

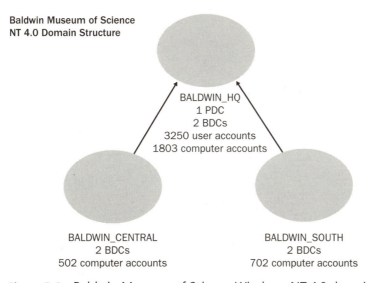

Figure 5-8   Baldwin Museum of Science Windows NT 4.0 domain structure

Currently, there are several computers running Windows NT 4.0 Workstation dispersed throughout the network. However, the company plans to upgrade all clients running operating systems prior to Windows 2000 to Windows XP Professional as soon as possible to take advantage of Group Policy. Your design plans should assume the following:

- All workstations in the BALDWIN_HQ domain are running Windows XP Professional.

- All workstations in the resource domains are running Windows 2000 Professional or Windows XP Professional.

Based on what you know about the organization, answer the following questions:

1. What types of trust relationships exist in the Windows NT 4.0 domain structure?

2. What additional information would you like to know about the physical equipment before discussing an upgrade or migration strategy?

3. How many forests are justified by what you know thus far? What more would you want to know before you make a recommendation?

4. How many domains are justified at this time? What additional information would you need to make a recommendation?

ACTIVE DIRECTORY AND NETWORK INFRASTRUCTURE DESIGN FOR TAILSPIN TOYS

Amy Lyon, the leader of the design team at Tailspin Toys, hires you as a consultant to help design a forest and domain infrastructure for the company. Amy tells you to first review the locations, administrative decisions, and acquisitions documents, as well as all the network diagrams that are located on your student CD in the Lab Manual\ReviewLabs folder. After you review these documents, Amy tells you the following:

"The Tailspin Toys management team has decided to aggressively pursue the acquisition of Fabrikam, Inc., in Istanbul, Turkey, and Trey Research, in Monterrey, Mexico. Given our many acquisitions in the past few years, and because we're hoping to acquire Fabrikam and Trey Research, we want to create an Active Directory design that fulfills the expanding international business needs of Tailspin Toys. But remember, we also need to satisfy our current IT requirements. I know that Ben Smith, the director of the Quality Assurance [QA] department, has some security concerns for his department that he wants to share with you. We need a solid design that will support the current business environment and scale for anticipated future growth."

Next, you meet with Ben Smith. He relays the following information:

"The QA department requires assurance of security on all resources. We cannot allow unauthorized access to any information contained within our environment; much of the data we store is sensitive, both internally and externally. The QA management team must have assurances that this data will remain under our control only. In addition, our department's personnel must have the ability to communicate with individuals throughout our enterprise and with our customers."

The first thing Amy would like you to do is to complete the Tailspin Toys Network Connectivity Report, Table A-1.

Table A-1   Tailspin Toys Network Connectivity Report

Company/ Subsidiary	Location/ City	Link Type/ Connected To	Percent Utilization	Number of Users	Number of Workstations
Tailspin Toys	New York				
Tailspin Toys	Fayetteville				
Tailspin Toys	Singapore				
Wingtip Toys	Dublin				
Wingtip Toys	Wicklow				
Contoso, Ltd.	Osaka				
Contoso, Ltd.	Kobe				
Trey Research	Istanbul				
Fabrikam, Inc.	Monterrey				

All server computers are expected to run some edition of Windows Server 2003. Most of the client computers run Windows XP Professional, but about 25 percent run older Windows operating systems. Windows 95 is running on about 10 percent of the client computers.

Based on what you know about the Tailspin Toys network, answer each of the following questions. Explain each answer you give.

1. How many forests does Tailspin Toys need?

2. How many domains does Tailspin Toys need in each forest?

3. What kind of trusts would you recommend for Tailspin Toys?

4. Sketch the forest, domain, and trust design that you recommend for Tailspin Toys.

5. You are assigned to create an IP address design for the Tailspin Toys network. The entire company is assigned the Class B address 131.107.0.0. However, the IP address space is subdivided already. You've been assigned an IP address space 131.107.32.0/19. How would you subdivide the IP address space that you've been given to provide sufficient IP addresses for Singapore, Fayetteville, and New York? The IP address space you provide for each location must allow for 20 percent growth and for 10 servers, 10 managed devices, and 10 router ports in each location.

LAB 6

PLANNING ACTIVE DIRECTORY SITES AND SERVER PLACEMENT

This lab contains the following exercises and activities:

■ Exercise 6-1: Designing Sites and Site Links

■ Exercise 6-2: Using the Active Directory Sizer

■ Exercise 6-3: Designing the Placement of Domain Controllers

■ Lab Review Questions

■ Lab Challenge 6-1: Designing for Replication Convergence

SCENARIO

You are a consultant hired by the Tailspin Toys company. Tailspin Toys is planning to move to Active Directory and has engaged you to help them design their Active Directory site topology and place the servers in the correct locations for performance and fault tolerance.

Tailspin Toys has 18,000 employees. Most of the employees work during the day shift, but 2,000 employees work a night shift. About 15,000 employees work at the corporate headquarters in Phoenix, Arizona. The other employees work at the branch offices as shown in Table 6-1.

Table 6-1 **Employees per Location**

Location	Number of Employees
Dallas	200
New York City	1000
Kansas City	1800

You have received the design documents for the Active Directory domain for Tailspin Toys. There will be approximately 200 organizational units (OUs) for user, computer, and group accounts. There are approximately 20,000 groups, with each user account belonging to approximately 10 groups. The administrative staff has estimated that they will begin using about 25 user properties per user.

Tailspin currently uses a third-party e-mail program and has no plans to move to Microsoft Exchange in the next year. However, they anticipate having approximately 5,000 contacts configured as objects in Active Directory.

They will use the default Account Policy settings when the domain is created. All client computers are DHCP enabled, with a default lease period of 8 days. The client computers are all Windows XP Professional computers. Each user has one computer. In addition to the client computers, the network includes approximately 2,000 computers running Windows 2000 and Windows Server 2003. The network does not include any Windows 9x or Windows NT computers.

Currently, about 10 new employees join the company each week, which equals the number of employees that leave the company. The administrators indicate that user properties don't change that often—only about 50 changes a week typically.

Tailspin Toys has an arrangement with a leading server producer. The typical server uses dual-processor 933 Xeon processors. The design documents also include the use of Windows Server 2003 computers as DNS servers that will be Active Directory–integrated. The network does not support any remote connections using dial-up or virtual private networks (VPNs). There are no plans for any other Active Directory–integrated applications at this time. Figure 6-1 shows the physical topology of Tailspin Toys.

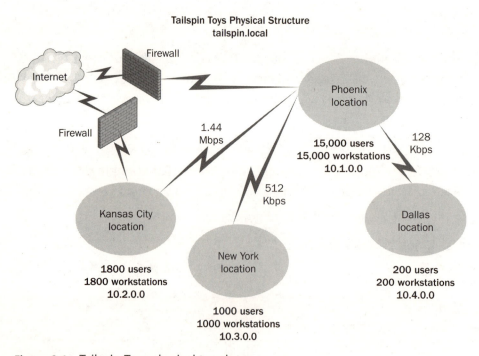

Figure 6-1 Tailspin Toys physical topology

After completing this lab, you will be able to:

■ Design sites

■ Identify site links

■ Use the Active Directory Sizer utility

■ Design the placement of domain controllers in sites

Estimated lesson time: 125 minutes

EXERCISE 6-1: DESIGNING SITES AND SITE LINKS

Estimated completion time: 25 minutes

You are asked to design the Active Directory site infrastructure based on the physical topology of Tailspin Toys. The WAN administrator for Tailspin indicates that he wants to reduce the amount of replication and authentication traffic over the WAN connections from Phoenix to New York and Dallas. For the WAN link between Phoenix and Kansas City, the network administrator wants to ensure that the amount of authentication traffic is kept to a minimum.

> **QUESTION** How many sites would you configure for Tailspin Toys, and what would you configure as the site links?

EXERCISE 6-2: USING THE ACTIVE DIRECTORY SIZER

Estimated completion time: 30 minutes

Using your answers to Exercise 6-1 and the information in the scenario, install and run the Active Directory Sizer to determine the number of domain controllers required and the size of the domain controllers that are suggested by the tool.

1. To install the Active Directory Sizer tool, run the file Setup.exe that is included in the Lab Manual\Lab06 folder on your student CD.

2. To run the Active Directory Sizer tool, click Start, point to All Programs, point to the Active Directory Sizer folder icon, and then click Active Directory Sizer. The Active Directory Sizer opens, as shown in Figure 6-2.

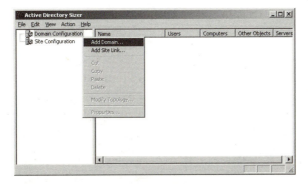

Figure 6-2 Active Directory Sizer

3. Right-click on Site Configuration, and then select Add Site Link.

4. Type **Phoenix-Dallas** for the Link Name and **128** for the Bandwidth, leaving Cost as **1**. Click OK.

5. Repeat steps 3 and 4 for the following site link names and bandwidths:

- ❑ Phoenix-New York; 512

- ❑ Phoenix-Kansas City; 1440

6. Right-click on Site Configuration, and then select Add Site.

7. Type **Phoenix** as the Site Name and **10.1.0.0** as the Subnet. Click OK.

8. Repeat steps 6 and 7 for the following site names and subnets (see Figure 6-3):

- ❑ Kansas City; 10.2.0.0

- ❑ New York; 10.3.0.0

- ❑ Dallas; 10.4.0.0

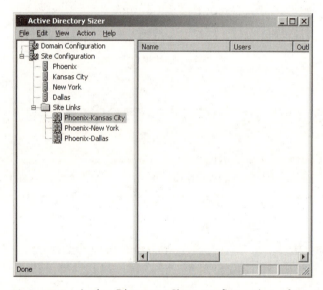

Figure 6-3   Active Directory Sizer configuration after step 8

9. Expand the Site Links node. Right-click on the Phoenix-Kansas City site link, and then select Modify Topology.

10. In the Sites Not In Link list, select Phoenix and Kansas City, and then select Add (see Figure 6-4) to add them to the Sites In Link list. Click OK.

11. Using the technique you learned in step 10, configure the Phoenix-New York site link to include only New York and Phoenix. Then modify the Phoenix-Dallas site link to include only the Phoenix and Dallas sites.

12. Right-click on Site Configuration, and then select Add Domain.

13. In the Please Enter A Domain Name box, type **Tailspin**.

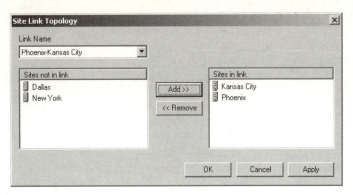

Figure 6-4   Site link topology configuration

14. Click Next, and then answer the questions displayed by the wizard based on the scenario and your answers in Exercise 6-1. As you answer each question, click Next to proceed. When you are finished answering questions, click Finished to receive your report.

15. Right-click on the Phoenix site, and then select Distribute Users.

16. In the Distribute Users window, select the Phoenix Source Site. Then, in the Users To Move box, enter **1800**. Then select the Kansas City Destination Site and click the Apply button.

17. In the Distribute Users window, select the Phoenix Source Site. Then, in the Users To Move box, enter **1000**. Select the New York Destination Site, and then click the Apply button.

18. In the Distribute Users window, select the Phoenix Source Site. Then, in the Users To Move box, input **200**. Select the Dallas Destination Site, and then click the Apply button.

19. Click OK and review the report.

> **QUESTION**   How many domain controllers were recommended? How many domain controllers per site?

EXERCISE 6-3: DESIGNING THE PLACEMENT OF DOMAIN CONTROLLERS

Estimated completion time: 20 minutes

The administrator reports to you that the company will be able to get nine servers to function as domain controllers until Active Directory is up and running for six months. This is an additional four domain controllers based on the output from Exercise 6-2.

The administrator still wants to maintain the desired replication and authentication reduction as specified in Exercise 6-1. He also says that he wants to ensure that users use the WAN link as seldom as possible when communicating with Active Directory.

> **QUESTION**   Where should you place the nine domain controllers based on this new information?

LAB REVIEW QUESTIONS

Estimated completion time: 20 minutes

1. Based on the output from the Active Directory Sizer tool in Exercise 6-2, how many additional domain controllers would you need if you added another three physical locations, each containing 2,000 employees?

2. What would change in your design from Exercise 6-1 if the following parameters changed?

   ❑ Four domain controllers

   ❑ WAN link between Phoenix and Kansas City was 512 Kbps

   ❑ WAN link between Phoenix and Dallas was 1.44 Mbps

3. If the administrator of Tailspin Toys decided not to use the universal group caching capabilities of Windows Server 2003, what would be your design for global catalog servers in Exercise 6-1? Answer by specifying how many global catalog servers there would be, as well as which domain controllers were configured as global catalog servers.

4. Please refer to Table 6-5 in Chapter 6 of the textbook, which details how many domain controllers are needed based on the number of user accounts. Using this table and the requirements in Exercises 6-1 and 6-3, how many domain controllers should Tailspin Toys have for the domain and sites?

5. You are informed that users often travel between the Phoenix office and the Kansas City office. Based on the design you configured for the sites and site links in Exercise 6-1, what would you suggest the replication interval be for the site link between Phoenix and Kansas City?

LAB CHALLENGE 6-1: DESIGNING FOR REPLICATION CONVERGENCE

Estimated completion time: 30 minutes

Tailspin Toys has decided to go with the site topology shown in Figure 6-5. You need to calculate the maximum time it will take to have a change on a domain controller in one site replicate to a domain controller in another site. What will the convergence time be for the following source and target domain controllers?

1. DC 5 to DC 6

2. DC 4 to DC 1

3. DC 1 to DC 9

4. DC 4 to DC 5

5. DC 4 to DC 7

6. DC 5 to DC 8

7. DC 10 to DC 1

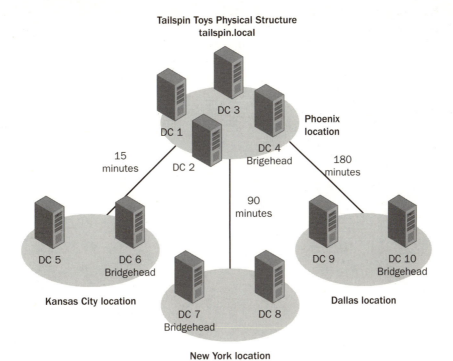

Figure 6-5   Site topology and replication intervals

LAB 7

DESIGNING AN ADMINISTRATIVE SECURITY STRUCTURE

This lab contains the following exercises and activities:

- Exercise 7-1: Creating an OU Design

- Exercise 7-2: Modifying OU Design to Support Group Policy

- Exercise 7-3: Delegating Administrative Authority

- Lab Review Questions

- Lab Challenge 7-1: Redesigning the OU and Domain Structure

SCENARIO

Northwind Traders manufactures a line of network appliances that are designed to help companies improve their data transmission capabilities. Northwind Traders currently uses a Microsoft Windows NT 4.0 master domain model. In recent years, the company has undergone significant growth and expansion. The company expects substantial growth over the next three years, including growth in market share, revenue, and the number of employees. In addition to opening two new offices, the executive management has committed to implementing a new Windows Server 2003 Active Directory design to meet the current and future needs of the company.

Table 7-1 shows the geographical locations, the departments residing in each location, and the number of users in each of the locations.

Table 7-1   **Northwind Traders Locations, Departments, and Users**

Location	Departments	Number of Users
Paris, France	Headquarters (HQ) Management Finance Sales Marketing Production Research Development Information Technology (IT)	2000
Los Angeles, CA, USA	Sales Marketing Finance IT	1000
Atlanta, GA, USA	Customer Service Customer Support Training	750
Glasgow, Scotland	Research Development Sustained Engineering IT	750
Sydney, Australia	Consulting Production Sales Finance	500

Northwind Traders already has a forest and domain design plan, which is illustrated in Figure 7-1.

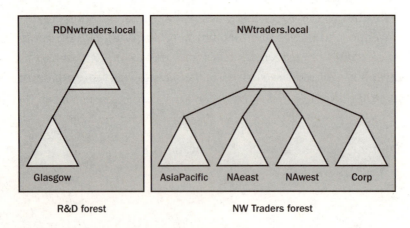

Figure 7-1   Forest and domain design

Table 7-2 illustrates where departmental user accounts are stored. For example, all personnel in the Sales department have their accounts in the NAwest domain.

Table 7-2   User Accounts by Department and Domain

Department	Domain
Sales	NAwest
Marketing	
Production	AsiaPacific
Research	Glasgow
Development	
Finance	Corp

After completing this lab, you will be able to:

■ Create the conceptual design of the organizational unit (OU) structure.

■ Identify Group Policy requirements for the OU structure.

■ Design an OU structure for the purpose of delegating authority.

■ Define the scope of a security group to meet requirements.

■ Specify account requirements for users, computers, administrators, and services.

■ Design the administration of Group Policy Objects (GPOs).

■ Design the deployment strategy of GPOs.

■ Create a strategy for configuring the user environment with Group Policy.

■ Create a strategy for configuring the computer environment with Group Policy.

Estimated lesson time: 110 minutes

EXERCISE 7-1: CREATING AN OU DESIGN

Estimated completion time: 25 minutes

Nancy Anderson, CIO of Northwind Traders, would like you to recommend a top-level organizational unit (OU) design based on the information you have about the company. Nancy wants you to use OU names that are representative of the users and departments. Complete Table 7-3 and then create a sketch to make your design suggestions.

Table 7-3   **Northwind Traders OU Design**

Domain	Top-Level Organizational Units
Corp.NWtraders.local	
NAwest.NWtraders.local	
NAeast.NWtraders.local	
Glasgow.RDNwtraders.local	
AsiaPacfic.NWtraders.local	

EXERCISE 7-2: MODIFYING OU DESIGN TO SUPPORT GROUP POLICY

Estimated completion time: 20 minutes

Nancy takes your suggested design to a meeting with the rest of the design team. You are unable to attend the meeting, but you do receive some feedback through Nancy. She writes you an e-mail that includes the following points:

- Executives in Paris require their laptops to have specific security settings that should not be applied to their desktop computers.

- All servers in the Finance department must use IPSec for all communications.

- All personnel in the Sales department must have a customer tracking application installed on their computers.

- All laptop computers in the Los Angeles location must have password-protected screen savers configured.

- All personnel in the Customer Support department who work in the call center have specific applications that must be installed on their computers.

- All computers in the Glasgow domain, even new computers that have just joined the domain, require an IPSec policy applied.

- All computers in the Research department require specific security settings.

- Multiple people on different shifts use computers in the Production department. These computers require specific desktop and user interface settings for users that log on to these computers.

Based on this information, Nancy asks whether you would make additions or modifications to the OU design you proposed to support these requirements. Assume that Active Directory and Group Policy will be used to enforce settings and deploy software wherever possible. What additional OUs would you create to support the additional requirements? Briefly write out your recommendations and modify the sketch you created in Exercise 7-1 as needed to match your recommendations.

EXERCISE 7-3: DELEGATING ADMINISTRATIVE AUTHORITY

Estimated completion time: 15 minutes

After approving the OU structure you recommended, Nancy asks you how her team should go about delegating administrative authority. She gives you the following examples of administrative requirements:

- Jeff Pike is part of the IT department in the Corp domain. He is responsible for all laptop computers at that location. He needs to be able to manage every aspect of laptop account objects.

- Susan Burk is the recently hired call center manager. She needs to be able to reset passwords for all user accounts that are members of Call Center.

- James Peters is a new administrator in Glasgow. He is responsible for managing and planning Group Policy for the Research, Development, and Sustained Engineering departments.

Complete Table 7-4 to define where user accounts should exist and to which OUs users should be delegated permission, as well as the permissions they should be given.

Table 7-4 **OU Delegations and User Accounts**

Employee	User Account Location, Domain/Container	Delegation OU	Permissions
Jeff Pike			
Susan Burk			
James Peters			

LAB REVIEW QUESTIONS

Estimated completion time: 20 minutes

1. How would you assign responsibility for managing Group Policy in each location of Northwind Traders, based on the scenario?

2. In Exercise 7-3, you were given names of specific users who needed to perform specific tasks for specific groups of objects. Assume now that each of those users hires two assistants to help perform the tasks. How might you change the delegation to handle present and future changes in the actual user accounts that need to perform those tasks?

3. Northwind Traders hires a group of auditors that require access to all the computers in each domain. What type of group would be most appropriate for these auditors? Where would the group reside?

4. If you learned that the NAwest and Corp domains were to be consolidated into the Corp domain, what changes might you make in the OU structure of the consolidated domain?

5. Northwind Traders hires Paul West to perform a similar function as James Peters performs. The difference is that Paul West is responsible for managing Group Policy for OUs in both NAeast and NAwest. How would you go about giving Paul West permissions to the appropriate OUs?

LAB CHALLENGE 7-1: REDESIGNING THE OU AND DOMAIN STRUCTURE

Estimated completion time: 30 minutes

Northwind Traders has sold its AsiaPacific operation as well as RDNwtraders. The company is now consolidating operations in North America. Company management wants to collapse the NWtraders forest so that it contains only two domains: Corp and NWtraders. Nancy provides the following information:

- Executive laptops will not have the same security requirements as laptops from other departments.

- The IT department will be consolidated into a single group and requires a different password policy than the rest of the departments.

- A new Production department was created and given 200 computers that require identical security configurations.

Create a new sketch of how the Northwind Traders network will look after this reorganization. Explain each modification.

LAB 8
DESIGNING AND SECURING INTERNET CONNECTIVITY

This lab contains the following exercises and activities:

- Exercise 8-1: Firewall and Perimeter Network Design

- Exercise 8-2: Virtual Private Network Design

- Exercise 8-3: Shared Internet Connectivity Design

- Lab Review Questions

- Lab Challenge 8-1: Enabling Secure LAN Access

- Lab Challenge 8-2: Expanding Distributor Services

SCENARIO

You are working as a directory design consultant for Coho Vineyard in Napa Valley, California. The vineyard has a medium-size Active Directory infrastructure at a single location. The Active Directory domain name is cohovineyard.com. There are two domain controllers on the network and three application servers. All servers run Windows Server 2003, Standard Edition. The network also has 500 client computers, all running Windows XP Professional. All client computers are members of the domain. The company uses Active Directory–integrated DNS, and both domain controllers run the DNS service.

The company has a dedicated T1 connection to the Internet, as shown in Figure 8-1. Internet connectivity is shared through a router with a T1 card that is maintained by the Internet service provider (ISP). The ISP manages the router as well as the 10.1.1.0/24 Dynamic Host Configuration Protocol (DHCP) scope configured on that router.

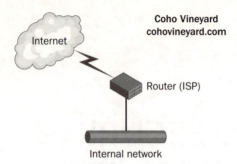

Figure 8-1   Overview of the Coho Vineyard network

Coho Vineyard has two additional routers separating the internal network, as shown in Figure 8-2. The domain controllers, servers, and client computers are distributed evenly among the segments. All segments and clients are connected by 100-Mbps Ethernet connections.

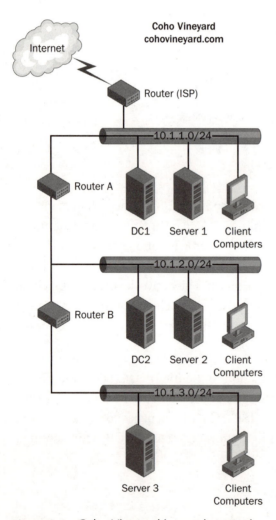

Figure 8-2   Coho Vineyard internal network

After completing this lab, you will be able to:

■ Design Internet connectivity for a company

■ Design a perimeter network

■ Design a virtual private network solution

■ Design a Network Address Translation (NAT) solution

Estimated lesson time: 110 minutes

EXERCISE 8-1: FIREWALL AND PERIMETER NETWORK DESIGN

Estimated completion time: 30 minutes

Coho Vineyard management wants to create a direct sales Web site and catalog for customers. They have increased the size of the IT department so it can handle these additional responsibilities.

The IT manager, Frank, has arranged to take over the administration of the WAN connection. The router that belongs to the ISP will be removed, but the T1 connection will remain onsite. Frank says that the responsibility for name resolution will also be delegated from the ISP to his department. He wants your help in designing a secure network for the Web server.

Frank wants to allow Internet users to access the Web server named www.cohovineyard.com, but he doesn't want them to be able to access internal network resources. He also wants internal network users to be able to access the Internet.

Frank has purchased two new Windows Server 2003 servers. One server is running Windows Server 2003, Web Edition, and the other server is running Windows Server 2003, Standard Edition.

Describe and sketch your proposed network design based on these requirements.

EXERCISE 8-2: VIRTUAL PRIVATE NETWORK DESIGN

Estimated completion time: 20 minutes

Coho Vineyard wine sales are limited to the Napa Valley and some select cities in Northern California. Over the past few years, the company has purchased additional land and thereby expanded its grape production capacity. However, the existing vineyard facilities are unable to handle the increased supply of grapes. In the past, excess grapes were sold to other wineries and grape juice drink producers. This year, in hopes of expanding sales outside Northern California, Coho Vineyard established a partnership agreement with an existing winery in San Diego, California (about 500 miles to the south).

The partner company will help to produce and distribute wine for Coho Vineyard. The partner company already has an Active Directory implementation. As part of this new alliance, the partner company has changed its company name to Coho Winery. The domain name cohowinery.com is already registered with the InterNIC. Last week, the Active Directory forest and domain of the partner company were renamed to cohowinery.com.

Currently, Coho Winery doesn't have a connection to the Internet. It does have a local network with about 200 computers. The network manager estimates that network bandwidth requirements will range from 500 Kbps to as high as 1.4 Mbps.

Coho Winery users need access to the inventory database that is maintained at Coho Vineyard. The inventory database is a custom application maintained on a Windows Server 2003, Standard Edition computer, named Inventory. Coho Vineyard management does not want the inventory database computer exposed directly to the Internet. Furthermore, management doesn't want unencrypted communications traversing the Internet when people from Coho Winery access the database.

What design can you recommend to allow users at Coho Winery access to this server, given these parameters? You are authorized to add one additional server computer to the network to allow access to the Inventory computer. You must also specify the type of Internet connection you recommend. Sketch and describe your answer.

EXERCISE 8-3: SHARED INTERNET CONNECTIVITY DESIGN

Estimated completion time: 10 minutes

Coho Vineyard recently purchased a small winery in Tuscany, Italy. Currently, the location has only one Windows Server 2003 computer and approximately 25 Windows XP Professional client computers. The location doesn't have an Internet connection, but company management wants similar connectivity in Tuscany as they have in San Diego. Unfortunately, none of the connectivity solutions offered in that location allow for multiple computer access to the Internet. Right now, the LAN is configured with an IP address range of 192.168.1.0/24. The local IT staff prefers to not have to modify their statically configured hosts.

You must design a connectivity solution that allows the client computers to access the Internet. Your design should not require the purchase of any additional servers. Be sure to discuss how you would modify the configuration to increase security. Describe your answer and add this office to your existing sketch.

LAB REVIEW QUESTIONS

Estimated completion time: 20 minutes

1. If Coho Vineyard has a perimeter network with a Web server and a DNS server, what do you do to allow internal network users access to the Web site?

2. What forest functional level is Coho Winery using for its Active Directory implementation?

3. If Coho Winery and Coho Vineyard are part of the same Active Directory domain (each with one or more domain controllers), what do you need to modify so that the two locations can replicate changes?

4. If the Tuscany office grows to exceed 300 computers and the existing Internet access is too slow, what type of design changes would you recommend?

5. Coho Vineyard has acquired a high-speed multiport switch, as well as three additional 10/100-Mbps switches. The company wants to implement a design that provides easy modularity and provides for future growth. How would you suggest they implement the new switches?

LAB CHALLENGE 8-1: ENABLING SECURE LAN ACCESS

Estimated completion time: 15 minutes

How would you reconfigure your network design if the Tuscany office requires secure data access to the LAN in San Diego as well as to the Inventory server in Napa Valley? Describe and sketch your answer.

LAB CHALLENGE 8-2: EXPANDING DISTRIBUTOR SERVICES

Estimated completion time: 15 minutes

You learn that both Tuscany and San Diego require secure access to the Inventory computer as well as to a new computer named Ordering. Both computers run Windows Server 2003. They have network cards but are not connected to the internal LAN. How do you modify your design to allow both locations to access the Ordering and Inventory computers? Describe and sketch your answer.

LAB 9
DESIGNING A STRATEGY FOR NETWORK ACCESS

This lab contains the following exercises and activities:

- Exercise 9-1: Designing Remote Connectivity

- Exercise 9-2: Planning Remote Access Policies

- Exercise 9-3: Wireless LAN Design

- Lab Review Questions

- Lab Challenge 9-1: Smart Cards for VPN Access

SCENARIO

Northwind Traders manufactures a line of network appliances that are designed to help companies improve their data transmission capabilities. Northwind Traders recently upgraded its Windows NT 4.0 master domain model to Windows Server 2003 Active Directory. The newly created Active Directory domain structure is shown in Figure 9-1.

The forest root domain is named nwtraders.com. The three domain controllers for nwtraders.com are physically located in a company building in Paris, France. However, nwtraders.com functions as an empty forest root domain. Table 9-1 lists the locations, domain names, number of domain controllers, and Active Directory site names.

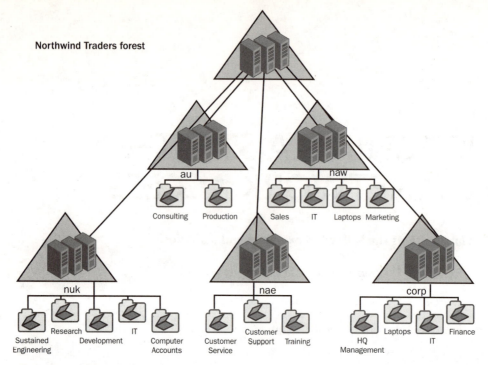

Figure 9-1   Domain and forest structure of Northwind Traders

Table 9-1   **Northwind Traders Locations, Domains, and Sites**

Location	Domain(s)	Site Names	Computers
Paris, France	nwtraders.com	PAR	3 Windows Server 2003 domain controllers
	corp.nwtraders.com		2 Windows Server 2003 domain controllers
			5 Windows Server 2003 server computers
Atlanta, Georgia, USA	nae.nwtraders.com	ATL	2 Windows Server 2003 domain controllers
Los Angeles, California, USA	naw.nwtraders.com	LA	2 Windows Server 2003 domain controllers
Sydney, Australia	au.nwtraders.com	SYD	3 Windows Server 2003 domain controllers
Glasgow, Scotland, UK	nuk.nwtraders.com	GLS	2 Windows Server 2003 domain controllers

Each location is connected as shown in Figure 9-2.

Each location uses Windows Server 2003 computers running Microsoft Internet Security and Acceleration (ISA) to connect to the other locations.

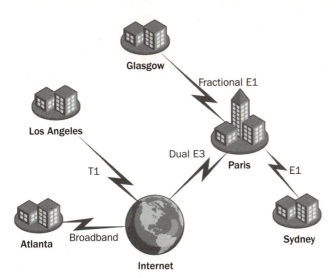

Figure 9-2   WAN connectivity diagram of the Northwind Traders network

The nwtraders.com and au.nwtraders.com domains have three domain control-lers each. Every other domain in the forest has two domain controllers. There is approximately one client computer for every network user in the company. In Glasgow, two computers are running Windows NT 4.0 Server and three comput-ers are running Windows Server 2003, Standard Edition. All other locations have three to five member servers running Windows Server 2003, Standard Edition. All server computers in each location are members of their local domain.

Table 9-2 describes the operating system type and number of client computers in each location.

Table 9-2   Type and Number of Client Computers by Location

Location	Client Computer OS Type	Number
Paris	Windows XP Professional	400
Atlanta	Windows 2000 Professional	650
Los Angeles	Windows 2000 Professional	750
Sydney	Windows 2000 Professional	700
Glasgow	Windows XP Professional	750
	Windows 2000 Professional	250
	Windows NT 4 Workstation	150
	Windows Me	75
	Windows 98, Second Edition	125
	Windows 95 OS Release 2	150

After completing this lab, you will be able to:

- Design secure remote access solutions
- Design remote access policies
- Design wireless connectivity

Estimated lesson time: 120 minutes

EXERCISE 9-1: DESIGNING REMOTE CONNECTIVITY

Estimated completion time: 30 minutes

You are a consultant who is assisting with the Northwind Traders network infrastructure design. You have a meeting with the CIO, Nancy Anderson, and a domain administrator from Glasgow, James Peters. The following situations and questions arise during the meeting.

1. Nancy tells you that she wants all company communications that traverse the Internet to be encrypted. She asks you to outline appropriate solutions as well as any potential obstacles to implementing these solutions, given what you know about the Northwind Traders network. Be sure to point out the most logical solutions for implementing encryption and the types of protocols that can be used. Discuss any upgrades that Northwind Traders should consider.

2. James tells you that all of the network administrators for the Glasgow domain have dial-up access to the network to allow for remote administration. The administrators use Windows XP Professional laptop computers to dial in to Windows NT 4.0 Remote Access Service (RAS) servers (Network Access Servers [NAS]). James also tells you that all of the Windows 95, Windows 98, and Windows Me computers in Glasgow are laptop computers. Traveling salespeople use these laptops to connect to the Glasgow domain over dial-up connections that they have with their personal Internet Service Providers (ISP). James tells you that he wants to increase the security of the domain and RAS servers, if possible. He also says that the company sales manager wants to reduce the cost of long-distance calls generated by the traveling salespeople connecting to the RAS severs from different countries.

   Outline James's options. Be sure to address cost-effective upgrades that would help achieve a higher level of security.

EXERCISE 9-2: PLANNING REMOTE ACCESS POLICIES

Estimated completion time: 30 minutes

You meet with the senior network administrator of the Los Angeles location, Robert Lyon. Robert tells you that there are three Windows Server 2003 computers configured as network access servers (NASs). Salespeople and network administrators use the NASs to connect to the network.

1. Robert explains that he has to grant or deny remote access permissions through each user account's properties sheet to control dial-in access. He wants to be able to use Windows Server 2003 remote access policies, but he is unable to select the Control Access Through Remote Access Policy option on the Dial-In tab of the user's account. What can Robert do to enable this option?

2. Now that you have solved the problem of enabling remote access policies, Robert wants to know how best to configure his NAS devices. He wants to enforce the same set of policies for each NAS. He also wants to implement centralized logging of remote connections. How do you suggest he configure his servers?

3. Robert wants to ensure that only domain administrators can connect remotely between the hours of midnight and 2 A.M. Pacific Standard Time. He also wants to ensure that dial-in connections can use only the highest possible level of Microsoft dial-in authentication without having to deploy certificates or smart cards. How does Robert implement these requirements?

EXERCISE 9-3: WIRELESS LAN DESIGN

Estimated completion time: 10 minutes

Nancy Anderson calls you in to discuss the Northwind Traders wireless infrastructure. She tells you that the corporate network in Paris uses Wired Equivalent Protocol (WEP) and MAC address restrictions to protect wireless access. In addition to increasing the security of the wireless network in Paris, network managers want to implement wireless connectivity in Glasgow, Sydney, Atlanta, and Los Angeles.

The new wireless design must meet the following criteria:

- Only employees should be able to connect to the company's wireless infrastructure. Visitors and anyone near any of the company locations should not be able to connect to it.

- The wireless network must be protected by the most secure method of encryption that is currently available.

Nancy passes on a few questions for you to answer to help Northwind Traders begin its wireless infrastructure design talks. Answer each question based on the requirements for the new wireless design.

1. Which method of authentication do you recommend for the Northwind Traders wireless implementation in each location?

2. Which encryption method do you recommend for the Northwind Traders wireless infrastructure?

3. What additional types of servers or network services are required to support the wireless design?

4. Are any hardware or software upgrades required?

LAB REVIEW QUESTIONS

Estimated completion time: 20 minutes

1. James Peters says that he needs all laptop computers in Glasgow to be able to dial up and that he wants to ensure that only MS-CHAP v2 is used for authentication. What changes do you recommend?

2. The CIO of Northwind Traders tells you that all client computers must support Group Policy. What changes to the Northwind Traders network do you recommend?

3. James Peters tells you that he must maintain dial-up access to his network, but he can replace no more than 200 of his client computers. He tells you that new computers he purchases can be desktops or laptops running Windows XP Professional. Assuming the older computers are also running the older operating systems, which computers can he replace to increase security? Explain your answer.

4. A new domain administrator in the Los Angeles office creates a policy that denies access to the Domain Users group when an asynchronous connection (modem) is used. The administrator then assigns this as the highest-priority policy on all NAS devices. Will this policy affect domain administrators who are trying to connect with asynchronous modems? Explain your answer.

5. A domain administrator in Glasgow does the following:

   ❑ Creates a remote access policy that specifies a Day-And-Time-Restriction policy that grants access 24 hours a day, 7 days a week.

   ❑ Configures the remote access policy profile so that MS-CHAP v2 is the only authentication protocol selected.

❑ Configures this remote access policy as number 1 in the order column.

❑ Creates another remote access policy that grants access 24 hours a day, 7 days a week. The remote access policy profile is not modified.

❑ Configures this remote access policy as number 2 in the order column.

What happens when a Windows 95 laptop user attempts a dial-up connection to the NAS?

LAB CHALLENGE 9-1: SMART CARDS FOR VPN ACCESS

Estimated completion time: 30 minutes

Northwind Traders is considering deploying smart cards throughout the enterprise to allow for VPN access. The company wants employees to be able to connect using the VPN from any location, using their smart cards regardless of which domain holds their user account. Describe the additional services, upgrades, and equipment that are required to implement such a change.

REVIEW LAB B

ORGANIZATIONAL UNIT AND NETWORK ACCESS DESIGN FOR TAILSPIN TOYS

You are a consultant who is helping to design a forest and domain infrastructure for Tailspin Toys. The company has decided to use the Active Directory design shown in Figure B-1.

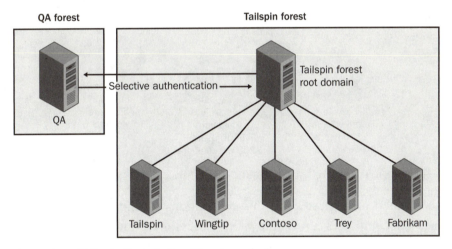

Figure B-1   Tailspin Toys Active Directory design

The WAN connectivity for the company's locations is depicted in Figure B-2.

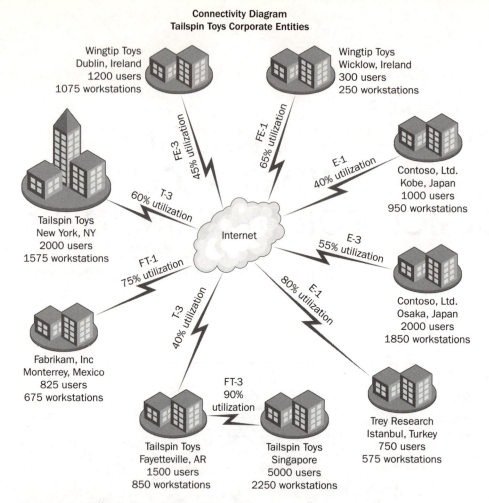

Figure B-2   Tailspin Toys connectivity diagram

All server computers are expected to run some edition of Windows Server 2003. Most of the client computers run Windows XP Professional, but about 25 percent run older Windows operating systems. Windows 95 is running on about 10 percent of the client computers.

Review the locations, administrative decisions, and acquisitions documents as well as all the network diagrams that are located on your student CD in the Lab Manual\ReviewLabs folder for more information about the company and its network infrastructure.

The design team leader, Brenda Diaz, needs you to start work on an Active Directory site design for the Tailspin Toys network that includes all of the company's subsidiaries and new acquisitions.

1. Create a sketch of the site design you recommend for Tailspin Toys and all of its subsidiary companies. Be sure to include the following in your sketch:

- Site name and local company name

- Location

- Number of users and number of workstations

- Connecting lines illustrating the site links and site link names

Brenda has had a meeting with upper management and the directors of all the departments in the company in which the decision was made to delegate control of the subsidiaries' networks to their existing IT personnel. She asks you to recommend an organizational unit (OU) design that will allow for distributed control of resources and also ensure that administration is as simplified as possible. She tells you to keep the following in mind as you design the OU structure:

- Each location has its own IT staff that needs some local authority.

- Each location except New York has a Budget office that handles local budgets and financial matters. New York has the Finance office, to which all Budget offices report.

- A custom application must be deployed only to site representatives (SiteReps) who work in the Sales offices in New York, Dublin, and Osaka.

- Quality Assurance has an office in each location, but its IT staff has the same needs in every location.

2. Sketch your proposed OU design. Be sure to indicate where you will place the IT staff for each location.

The security administrator tells you that the company has many people in the field who need ready access to resources. The company used to maintain direct dial-up servers so that the traveling sales force could access Tailspin's internal network with their portable computers. To reduce costs, Tailspin recently decided to outsource all dial-up connectivity to an international ISP. The sales force now has Internet access, but Tailspin needs to implement VPN servers to enable the sales team to access the internal network securely.

Tailspin needs a complete VPN solution and also needs to know how to efficiently reconfigure employees' portable computers to access the new dial-up ISP and to connect to the VPN servers. It also needs options for making remote access as secure as possible.

The security administrator has been asked to provide high-speed wireless access with high security. The CEO is eager to deploy wireless access to all locations at Tailspin Toys—this will especially help the employees who travel from office to warehouse to factory during the day.

One of the CEO's requirements is that clients who visit Tailspin offices must be able to access the Internet via the wireless network. However, these clients must not be able to access the internal network. Wireless network traffic can easily be sniffed by nearby workstations. The security administrator says that previously, people were able to sniff wireless traffic from the parking lot. The new wireless solution must be as secure as possible to avoid such problems.

3. Specify a complete VPN solution for Tailspin Toys that meets all these requirements.

4. Specify a solution to efficiently reconfigure employees' portable computers to access the new dial-up ISP and to connect to the VPN servers.

5. What other recommendations can you make to improve remote access security?

6. Create a wireless access design that avoids the security problems of previous implementations at Tailspin Toys. The design must ensure that clients who visit the offices of Tailspin Toys can access the Internet by using the wireless network, but it must prevent these clients, along with other unauthorized wireless users, from accessing the internal network.